SocializeWith.Me

Or Someone Else Will

Gaspare J. Marturano

See you online!

@GASPAREM

Gaspare J. M.

SocializeWith.Me (Or Someone Else Will)

First Edition

Designed By: Ben Hoffman

Editor: Dr. P J George
Associate Professor of English, St Dominic's College

ISBN-13: 978-1460975374

ISBN-10: 1460975375

Lisa, Isabel and Joshua
Mom, Dad, Lina and Marc
Gail and Allen
My family/My world.
To All My Friends, Followers, and Contacts
For my grandfather Gaspare Marturano, who I know is
watching down over me every day.

"There has been a fundamental shift in the way
we communicate today." – Unknown

Foreword

As I sit here in New York City thinking about social media, it strikes me that ten years ago a book solely dedicated to this topic would not have been written. Now you've picked this book up (or bought it electronically), and will have gone through the history of social media by the time you finish the last chapter.

How "fast" is social media? About a year ago, I was hosting an IRL ("In Real Life") social media event in New York City. It was a meet and greet for mommy bloggers – and it was meant to be a casual walk around and meet others event – no real sitting and talking, just cocktail tables for resting your drinks on. One mommy blogger was in her last term of pregnancy, and evidently couldn't believe that chairs had not been provided for the guests. Instead of hailing one of the hosts of the event, she tweeted that this poorly run event was not taking care of its guests. My Atlanta office was monitoring the social media chatter and noticed this post immediately in NYC – and we attempted to find the person who posted the tweet. It wasn't long before her tweet was re-tweeted again and again, taking on a life of its own. How did this get resolved? Old school. One of our team members stood on a chair and proclaimed, "Who here would like a chair?" The woman raised her hand and a chair was delivered. I then asked her to tweet out to the world that she was "OK". How long did this entire process take? *About 5 minutes.*

Whether you are reading this book as an individual or as part of an organization, the tips and tactics on the following pages will save you valuable time and money. The example recounted above happens every day, and information moves faster and faster as new social media platforms are created and mature. New and old school tactics continuously blend and evolve. I find myself using business tactics from pre-social media days with new platforms.

One of my clients, a large university in Southern California, is hosting a conference this Spring. The challenge is how to spread the word about the conference to key demographics? What can we do that hasn't been done a million times before? Send a spam email? (No, no thank you). Our team pulled an old-school tactic and married it to a (very) new social media tactic: Garage sale poster rip-off tab sheet meets QR code (A QR code is a new type of bar code, which can be scanned by most smartphones). You've seen them in break rooms, laundromats, poles on the side of the road – right? Simply put, we placed a large QR code on an 8 ½" x 11" sheet of paper, then approximately 10 smaller versions of the code on small rip-off tabs at the bottom of the poster. When scanned, the users' phone took them to a special Facebook page where they could learn about the event. The tabs themselves became social media messengers, traveling around the campus of the university where it was posted.

The combination of old-school and modern platforms, or different kinds of modern platforms, is happening every day. The challenge is to remember what your goal is and create a tactic which maps to that goal.

Sometime, somewhere, someone is going to ask, "Where did that money (or time) go that we spent on the 'social media project'"? I always want to be able to answer with certainty, listing the goals we set out to meet, followed by the tactics and platforms used, then the results.

A lot of people gravitate to Twitter as THE social media platform to bring their company success. As you'll see in the chapters that follow, it's only one of hundreds of platforms. Be open minded and use platforms that help you meet your goals.

Recently a CEO of a large television broadcasting company asked me why his social media 'plan' wasn't working for his organization. I asked what he was doing in the space. He answered, "I told my sales team to go out and start tweeting!" He had no goal, no plan, and in fact missed one of the fundamental keys to using social media correctly – watch out for your brand. Your brand is important. My brand is important. There are companies in the world who have spent millions, if not billions, of dollars building their brand's image, yet place the social media charter in the hands of an untrained intern (true story, by the way). I work hard to build a consistent brand for my company in social media; I also concurrently work on the brand for Brian Boyd.

Has this ever happened to you – you meet a friend or colleague who you haven't seen in a long time and they begin telling you everything *you've* been doing lately? They've probably been following your stream on Facebook and/or Twitter. Every time that happens to me I'm taken back. That's my brand being put out there. You can control your brand. Hold it carefully – you can mold it and shape it to be what you want it to be. Have a plan; don't leave it as a second thought.

I'm honored to be a part of SocializeWith.Me – the book, the experience, the brand. Mr. Marturano has succinctly gathered years of research, intellectual property, tips and tricks into an easy-to-carry package (this book!). Keep this handy – and pull it out in your next meeting or coffee break. You'll look like you've been studying social media for years.

I challenge you to take what you learn here and begin building your brand or the brand of your organization – use the power for good, not evil. ☺

Brian E. Boyd, Sr. - @brianboyd
President, Media Connect Partners, LLC

TABLE OF CONTENTS

Chapter One

A Brief History of Social Media

Social media is an obvious force in the modern world. It's used by both the average person and by businesses, from your Uncle Joe to Fortune 500 companies, and everyone in between. Although you might think that social media is a new phenomenon, actually it has a pretty rich history.

It is both older and newer than you might think. In this chapter, we'll touch on some of the high points in the history of social media, so that you can get an overview of how it started, how it's evolved since the early days and where it might be going in the future.

In the Dim and Misty Past

You might think that social media started with MySpace (it was during its rise in popularity that people really began to hear the buzz term "Social Media" in mainstream news), or with another rather recently released network site. You would be forgiven for thinking so, but social media actually started long before the first piece of glitter ever decorated a MySpace theme. In fact, it started even before the "Internet" itself started.

One of the earliest precursors to what we know today as social media were the usenets of the late '70s and early '80s. However, these were very different, and were more closely related to newsreaders and RSS feeds (important tools in the world of social media). Online "groups" – such as Yahoo! Groups – are also the direct descendants of these.

Bulletin board systems (BBSs) also came out about the same time. These were essentially private servers that connected via phone lines. While there was no commercially available Internet, BBS users could dial into a BBS using their modem. Most systems were limited to one user at a time, though there were some that could host a handful of users via advanced phone systems.

BBSs were the first platforms that allowed users to interact with each other, albeit on a limited basis. I ran my first BBS using a Commodore 64 and a 1200 baud modem, with two floppy drives. Yikes. It was dreadfully slow, but it served its purpose at the time. Keep in mind that these were the days before "unlimited" calling plans (I'm still paying my parents back for a phone bill from 1987).

The Birth of Online Services

After BBSs and usernets, online services like Prodigy and CompuServe came into existence. Actually, CompuServe dates back to the 1960s, though it was not really a viable option for most people to use (thanks to the enormous price tag). However, the rise of services like AOL and Prodigy gave many people their first chance to enter the online world.

Most of the social interaction with these systems came in the form of chat rooms and private chats – things that can still be found today. You only have to visit Yahoo! Chat to get a glimpse of what the world was like in those early days. Chat hasn't changed much, though the ability to interact has improved considerably.

There were even some limited attempts to offer shopping and gaming through these early online systems, though modern computer users would have found the systems unrecognizable. On my YouTube channel (youtube.com/gasparem), I have a link to Vintage Q-Link (AOL) Promotion Video from 1986. It provides a fascinating look at the roots of what we know today, as modern Social Media interaction.

Chat Goes Siteless

The hallmark of chat for many years was the need to log into a chat room or website to interact with others. However, with the birth of ICQ and IRC, that was no longer necessary. Instant messaging was born, in a form that most people would recognize today. ICQ was the first program designed for PCs that allowed instant messages between users without a need for a website or chat room.

While these tools might not be what you think of when you think about social media, they are responsible for many of the things that we know and love (or hate) about using modern social media sites. Avatars were introduced here, and emoticons were also developed during this time. Even "chat speak" or "lolspeak" was born here, with abbreviations like "LOL", "BRB" and "AFK" coming into general use.

Social Media You Can Recognize

While all of those things listed above were the forerunners and ancestors of social media, there are some other tools and platforms that might be a bit more recognizable to you. Dating websites (which have been around in one form or another almost from the beginning), are some of the direct progenitors of today's social media sites.

Forums, which are still used all over the place today, are also part of the social media movement, and they allowed users to connect, send messages, share content and do many more similar things in the days before Facebook and Twitter. However, if you want to find a true social media site from "back in the day," then you need to look no farther than LiveJournal.

LiveJournal is still around, and got its start back in the last century (1999). This platform was (and still is) based on sharing your life via a constantly changing blog, allowing your connections and friends to stay up to date by reading about your life.

In contrast, SixDegrees (another very early social network), allowed you to have a profile, but it was static, and did not change.

The 2000s – The Heyday of Social Networks

The 2000s brought more changes and innovations in the field. During those days, Friendster opened up. (Interestingly, it is still active, with 90 million users. It is now marketed as the "social gaming destination of choice"). You'll also find Hi5 (marketed as "social entertainment for the youth market worldwide" with

50 million monthly users) introduced during this time. For those who are well-connected in their professional life, LinkedIn (one of the most powerful forces in the social media world), was launched in May 2003. LinkedIn was one of the first social networks I joined. It took me years to build my contact list, and today I run the largest Maritime Network with well over 12,000 members.

In fact, the 2000s marked the birth of some of the most recognizable social media sites still in use. MySpace revolutionized the way people interacted, starting back in 2003. For several years, MySpace was the dominant force in this realm, though it has since lost that status and dropped several places in the online hierarchy (now number 32 in the U.S. according to Alexa.com).

2004 saw the birth of Facebook. It was very limited at the time, as it was only for Harvard students. However, by 2006, it was opened for everyone. Today, Facebook has risen to the #1 slot and is the world's largest (and most popular) social network with over 500 million users (http://on.fb.me/eWfo6L).

Facebook has several key differences when compared to networks like MySpace, the most notable being the lack of profile customization, though this does not seem to have harmed the network in any way.

The Modern Social Network Landscape

Today, there are almost as many social networks and niche social media sites as there are different reasons to use these platforms. Photobucket has become enormously popular, as has Tumblr, and Posterous, though these are not "social networks" per se. Rather, they are social media sites, a term that is a bit harder to define.

If you were to use one word to describe today's social media/network landscape, "fragmented" might come to mind. There are so many different options that it can take a long time to figure out what each one is about and whether or not you really want to use it. The big 3 of social networking are easily identified, though:

- **Facebook (obviously) -** More than 500 million active users; 50% of them log on to Facebook on any given day/ average user has 130 friends/ people spend over 700 billion minutes per month on Facebook/ there are more than 200 million active users currently accessing with their mobile devices/ people who use Facebook on their mobile devices are twice as active as non-mobile users (Stats - http://on.fb.me/eWfo6L).

- **Twitter (interestingly)** - Twitter now has 105,779,710 registered users/new users are signing up at the rate of 300,000 per day/180 million unique visitors come to the site every month/ 75% of Twitter traffic comes from outside Twitter.com (i.e. via third party applications.)/ Twitter gets a total of 3 billion requests a day via its API/ Twitter users are, in total, tweeting an average of 55 million tweets a day/ Twitter's search engine receives around 600 million search queries per day/ Of Twitter's active users, 37 percent use their phone to tweet/ over half of all tweets (60 percent) come from third party applications. (Stats - http://read.bi/dFrojw).

- **LinkedIn (not so oddly)** - LinkedIn operates the world's largest professional network on the Internet with more than 90 million members in over 200 countries and territories/more than half of LinkedIn members are located outside of the United States/ there were nearly two billion people searches on LinkedIn in 2010/ 90m+ professionals around the world as of January 2011/ more than one million companies have LinkedIn Company Pages (formerly known as company profiles)/ LinkedIn is currently available in six languages: English, French, German, Italian, Portuguese and Spanish /LinkedIn started off 2011 with about 1,000 full-time employees located all around the globe, up from around 500 at the beginning of 2010 (Stats - http://bit.ly/eHMhaj).

Actually, MySpace still ranks high, though they drop lower every day. Technically speaking, MySpace is probably ranked as #3 in most people's books, simply because LinkedIn is dedicated to connecting professionals, entrepreneurs and business owners, rather than being a "general" social network.

What are some of the other popular social networks out there? Here are some that you may or may not be familiar with:

- MyLife.com (formerly Reunion.com)

- Ning.com (once free now a paid service)

- LiveJournal (still alive and kicking!)

- Last.fm (a mixture of music and social networking)

- Hi5 (claims to be "the world's largest social entertainment destination")

- Meetup (offline group meetings in various localities around the world)

- BEBO (the site's name is an acronym for *"Blog Early, Blog Often"*)

- Netlog (formerly known as Facebox and Bingbox), is a Belgian social networking website specifically targeted at the European youth.

There is a very good chance that you probably haven't heard of some of those listed above. If so, don't feel bad. There are hundreds of different social media/network sites out there, and not all of them are right for you.

However, the best way to find the perfect platform is to experiment a bit. Just use caution when doing so – not all sites take your security as seriously as others, and providing too much information about yourself can be potentially harmful (a rule that you should apply to **ALL social networks**).

The Future of Social Media

The current trend in social media is one of greater interconnectivity. You'll see this in action anytime you notice a "like" button on a blog post (which allows you to "like" that post on Facebook). You can see this in the "tweet this" buttons on websites and blogs, as well. In fact, the ever-growing interconnectedness of the various social media sites has become quite extensive.

Facebook has initiated numerous things here – from their Facebook Connect, which allows you to use your Facebook ID to log into other services to their ubiquitous "like" buttons. For those following such things (and YOU should be), this trend is set to continue. In fact, social media will be the predominant means through which consumers like us find news, learn about companies and products, and ingest information.

When was the last time that you saw a news headline on a friend's Facebook status, clicked the link and actually read the story? Well, it might have been pretty recently. Would you have read that story if your "friend" had not posted the link? Probably not; therefore, you can already see how social media is changing the ways in which we get our information.

Of course, there are some distinctions to be drawn here, between social networks and social media, though those lines are getting increasingly blurred every day. Social network is a term generally applied to sites like Facebook, Twitter and LinkedIn – they're websites that you log into and share information with your connections.

Social media is a much broader term, which can be applied to an incredible array of sites and services. Most social networks are social media sites as well, but not all social media can be considered social networks. Take Posterous for instance. This is a new form of blogging that does not require you to fill out a lengthy profile or follow tedious steps like you do with Blogger or WordPress.

Posterous can be considered social media, because it allows you to share information with others and interact with friends, readers and other people. However, it is not necessarily a social network, because it differs considerably from the likes of Facebook, Twitter and LinkedIn.

In the rest of this book, you'll learn more about using social media: how it can be of use to you, what tools are available, and what strategies are offered to maximize its value to you, whether you are a private user or want to boost the growth of your business.

Chapter Two

Tools, Tools, Tools

As you can see from the information in the previous chapter, social media is here to stay. In addition, the number of social media/networks available to the average consumer, entrepreneur and business owner have increased dramatically in a pretty short time.

To make the best use of these sites and services, you're going to need some tools. This chapter will highlight those tools for you, and help you understand where, when, why and how to use them.

Knowledge – The Most Powerful Tool of All

Before we delve into the different services and apps that help you work with social media more easily, you need the most powerful tool of all – knowledge. Specifically, we need to address a common misconception. This was hinted at in the last chapter when it was mentioned that social networks are social media sites, but not all social media sites are social networks.

Social media is a very broad term that can be applied to almost anything it seems. Before you leap headlong into using these tools (more than you have already), it's a good idea to know what social media is, where social networks fall in that morass and, generally, to know more about these tools. Let's start with a rundown of the basic types of social media out there and a description of each.

Multimedia

Multimedia social media sites allow users and creators of media to connect in new and interesting ways. You'll find all types of sites out there for different purposes, including the following:

- **Music and Audio –** Pandora, Last.fm, The Hype Machine, Groove Shark, SoundCloud

- **Photography and Art –** deviantArt, Photobucket, BetweenCreation, Flickr, Tumblr

- **Video Sharing –** YouTube, Dailymotion, Vimeo, Metacafe, Openfilm, Sevenload

- **Presentations –** SlideShare, scribd

- **Livecasting –** JustinTV, Skype, Ustream, Livestream

Collaboration

Collaborative social media sites give you the ability to work with others, no matter where they are in the world. This category also contains social media sites designed to help you build your "authority" or "expertise" on different subjects by becoming an expert.

- **Social News –** Digg, Reddit, Mixx

- **Social Bookmarking –** StumbleUpon, Google Reader, Del.icio.us, Folkd, Diigo

- **Document Managing –** Docs.com, Google Docs

- **CMS (Content Management Systems) –** WordPress, custom CMS within your website

- **Wiki Solutions –** Wikimedia, Wikispaces, Wetpaint, Jottit

- **Social Navigation –** Waze, Trapster (web-based navigation and alerts for travel in the real world)

Communication

Most of what people consider social media falls into the communication category. Here, you will find everything from blogs to social networks, and everything in between. These tools help you communicate with friends and family, with customers and clients, as well as with business prospects.

- **Microblogging** – Twitter, Tumblr (blogging and photos), Yammer, Posterous, Foursquare, FMyLife, Identi.ca, Plurk, Jaiku

- **Social Networks** – Facebook, LinkedIn, Ning, Plaxo, Cyword, Orkut, Hyves, XING, Tagged, Formspring, MySpace, Hi5

- **Blogging** – Blogger.com, WordPress.com, LiveJournal, Open Diary, Xanga, TypePad

- **Online Fundraising** – Kickstarter, Causes, FirstGiving, RaiseItNow

- **Geo Social Networks** – Foursquare, The Hotlist, Facebook Places, Gowalla, GeoMati

- **Events** – The Hot List, Meetup.com

Consumer Reviews, Information and Opinions

These types of social media sites allow people to share information and opinions on multiple subjects, from companies to services to brands and more. People can also use these services to ask questions and tap into the immense knowledgebase represented by Internet users.

- **Questions and Answers –** eHow, Yahoo! Answers, WikiAnswers, Askville, Formspring

- **Reviews and Information –** Yelp, Customer Lobby, Epinions.com, Formspring

These are only a handful of the myriad social media sites out there, but you can see from this small segment just how vast and pervasive social media has become. It has implications for every area of your life.

There are others, like GetGlue, that span many different categories, as well as those like Google Guru that have lived brief lives and then moved on to the great social media graveyard. Now that you know a bit more about what social media is, where social networks fit into the area as a whole, and what users can do with these platforms, it's time to move on to other tools.

The Big 3 – Facebook, Twitter and LinkedIn

No discussion of social media tools can be complete without at least touching on the Big 3 social networks. For personal users, these will form the cornerstone of social networking efforts. The same can be said for business users, as the people you want to do business with will be found on these social networks. And, as any good business owner knows, you have to be where your customers are.

We'll start the discussion at the logical launching point – Facebook, the largest and most popular social network in the world.

Facebook (Facebook.com)

Facebook has been around so long that most people have heard of it, even if they've never used it before. This social network boasts more than 500 million users around the world for an average of 700 billion minutes spent on it each month.

Unlike LinkedIn, Facebook is about connecting people from all walks of life, whether you're coworkers, friends, family or just acquaintances. You can post status updates from your account, leave comments on the status updates and messages of your friends and so on.

Using Facebook also allows you to share photos, videos, music and more – in fact, you can share just about anything with your friends, and you can connect with just about anyone, whether that's a person or a company.

When most people think of social networking, Facebook is what they think of. It's not really about blogging, nor is it solely about one-to-one interaction, though that is a definite theme here. If you could sum up the purpose of Facebook into a single sentence, it would be something like, "Connecting all aspects of your life with new friends and old, family and coworkers, all around the world."

Twitter (Twitter.com)

Twitter is the rising star of the social network scene. In the past few months, it has quadrupled its growth (Facebook has doubled theirs). However, Twitter is very unlike Facebook in the way it is used and what you can do on it. While Facebook gives you a full profile in which to post details of your life, your likes and dislikes and share information with friends, Twitter limits you to a single sentence profile and 140 character tweets.

Then why is this network growing so quickly? Simply put, Twitter allows you to interact with others on a one-to-one or a group basis, in real time. Facebook lets you do something similar, but it is usually not in real time. Twitter has a "conversational" flavor that Facebook does not have.

In fact, it is this very conversational nature that makes Twitter such an excellent option for both private individuals looking to interact with real people and companies seeking to communicate with their audience, enhance their brand and so on.

LinkedIn (LinkedIn.com)

LinkedIn is one of the older social networks out there, and it is nowhere near as large as Facebook. However, that is not due to a lack of value or worth. Rather, it is because LinkedIn is a network dedicated to business professionals, entrepreneurs, business owners and the like. This is a professional network, designed to help you make connections in your professional life.

Networking has become increasingly important for businesses of all sizes. Of course, it is also vital for entrepreneurs and those seeking to shift to a different career.

The old axiom, "it's who you know" is very true in today's world.

LinkedIn helps you make the connections that you need so that you know the people you need to. You won't find games and puzzles here, as you will on Facebook. You won't find conversational messages (much) the way you will on Twitter. What you will find is a growing, popular social network that can connect companies and individuals together for the benefit of both.

Websites

The most common way to access social media sites is to actually visit the website itself. For instance, you can simply point your browser toward Facebook.com, log in and then start interacting with your friends and connections.

Using websites offers several advantages over other means (which will be covered shortly). For instance, the website usually offers more tools and more capabilities than you will find with other methods (though this is not always the case!). Using the service's website also makes it easier to accomplish a number of other things. These include the following:

- More screen real estate – Whether you're using a mobile app or a third-party app that combines different social networks, you will find that the website gives you more screen real estate. Often, this can help you have a better experience, allowing you to see all the details, suggestions, information and so on.

- Selecting contacts/friends – You'll also find that using the website interface for many of these services makes it simpler to choose the friend, follower or contact that you want to interact with. For instance, Facebook makes it pretty simple to choose which friend you want to message to.

- Managing other pages – While Facebook might be the most visible social media site to give you the ability to have more than one page, there are others. Using the website interface makes it simpler to manage those other pages, whether they are personal, professional or something else entirely.

- Hints/suggestions – Several social media sites (Twitter, Facebook and the like) give you suggestions and hints about potential new connections (friends and followers). Using the website interface is the best way to see these suggestions. These suggested connections are not always right, but they can be valuable tools, helping you find those you want to connect with.

However, that does not mean that you should only use the websites of these services. There are some drawbacks to using only the web interface.

- Computer access – The single largest drawback to using a web interface is that you have to have computer access. This might be your desktop, a laptop, netbook or even a tablet computer, but you have to have a web browser and a screen large enough to really make use of the web interface. Obviously, you're not at your computer 24-7.

- Missing tools/functionality – While most web interfaces give you a lot of power, there are some that leave things out, or never build them in to begin with. The best example of this is Twitter. While the "new Twitter" offers better functionality than their older interface, there are still some powerful tools missing that you can only access through third-party apps.

- Speed – Often, you will find that loading your browser and hitting your favorite social media/network site is a bit slower than using a third-party app. Apps for smartphones can give you immediate access just by tapping an icon on your screen (or pushing a button if you don't have a touch screen).

- Multitasking – Another huge issue with using web interfaces is that you cannot really multitask. Even having multiple browser windows open to the sites that you are using can be time consuming and difficult. Third-party apps are available that allow you to post, share and interact on multiple platforms at the same time.

Phone Apps

From the discussion above, observant readers have probably already guessed the next tools to make the list. Phone apps offer some pretty decent benefits, though they do have their drawbacks, as well. With the explosion of smartphone technology today, it seems as if everyone has access to the Internet on the go.

Of course, that access is via a small screen – even the vaunted iPhone and Android devices can't compare to using a computer monitor. Still, there are worse things than using your phone to connect to your social media sites.

It seems there are tons of different phone apps out there that allow you to connect to social networks. For example, there are tons of different apps for the iPhone, Android, and there are quite a few for Blackberry phones, as well. Other manufacturers have not been left out of the loop, either – you'll find an app that works on your phone with just a bit of research on whatever passes for your brand's "app store."

Using a phone app ensures that you are able to post status updates and interact with friends and family (or customers) while you're on the go (I use Ping.FM for my Android). You can accomplish many of the same things via social network specific apps (Facebook, Twitter, LinkedIn, etc.), though you will not necessarily have the same ease of use that you enjoy when using the web interface.

You will also have access to third-party apps for different social media sites depending on your phone and its capabilities. Some of the most popular third-party developers have released phone clients for their users that allow the same functionality that users enjoy with their desktop versions.

Using phone apps certainly has some drawbacks, though. It's a bit more difficult to navigate through the sites, depending on your phone and its capabilities. While users of iPhones, Android or touch screen Blackberry phones will have less trouble than those without touch screen technology (except for those with large, fat fingers like me), even those advanced devices are a bit limited.

Still, phone apps are an invaluable addition to your social media tools – they can help you remain connected when you have no computer access. For those who don't have a computer of their own, these apps can be the only way to get into social media.

Desktop Apps

As has been hinted at in this chapter, there are ways in which you can access multiple social media sites at the same time, interacting with your friends, posting new content and so on. Multiple desktop apps give you the ability to do things faster and better than working through web interfaces alone. What are the key benefits of these apps?

- Post to multiple social networks at once – One of the best things about these apps is the fact that you can post content to multiple social media sites and networks at the same time. A single post can be put on Twitter, Facebook, LinkedIn, Google Buzz, Foursquare, etc., with just the click of a button.

- Access to multiple streams at once – Another benefit of using desktop apps from third-party developers is that you can view more than one stream at a time. Consider Twitter as an example.

  Using the web interface lets you see your timeline, your @mentions, your direct messages and even retweets, but not all at the same time. However, using a desktop app you can see each of these streams in real-time, at the same time. You can also see streams from your other social networks, so that you are never left out of the conversation.

- More tools – In addition to giving you access to more information at one time, you will find that many desktop apps offer you more tools and better functionality than the web interface. Once again, let's use Twitter as our example here.

Retweeting is an important part of being a responsible "Twitizen." Twitter lets you retweet the tweets of others, but does not let you modify those tweets. Using a third-party app, you can retweet those messages as they are, or you can add your own comment to the tweet. Of course, you can access multiple tools and functions for all of your integrated social network accounts, not just Twitter.

- No need for browsers – You'll also find that using desktop apps negates the need to have your browser open to the web interface. This allows you to use your browser for other things while the app runs in the background, or to keep it closed if you prefer.

It can be confusing to have multiple tabs or windows open in your browser, and using an app can help you eliminate that frustration (Who hasn't accidentally closed out the wrong tab and then groaned in aggravation?).

- Better organization – For anyone using social media, staying organized is vital. However, if you are using it for your business, then it is vital. Using the web interface for a social network can be difficult when you are trying to market your company, interact with your customers and promote your business.

However, using a third-party app allows you to customize your feeds as you see fit, follow specific users and so on. There is no better way to maximize the value of social media and social networking for business users than to harness the potential of third-party apps.

So, what apps are worth your time? Which ones offer the best multi-network integration and the most tools? There are several excellent options out there, and you'll find that a bit of experimenting is the best way to choose one that works for you. It also depends on what platform you are using as well – PC, tablet, netbook, etc.

In the next section, we'll take a look at some of the better third-party social media apps and what they offer.

The Best Third-Party Desktop Apps for Social Media

As mentioned, there are tons of different apps out there. They're not all the same, though and some stand head and shoulders above the rest in terms of aesthetics, functionality, usability, multitasking, etc. What are the better solutions for your needs? There are three that come to mind immediately:

- TweetDeck

- HootSuite

- Seesmic

Each of these offers some serious benefits, and solid performance. In this section, we'll delve deep into each one and see just why you might want to use them for your social networking. Screenshots have been included so that you can get a good view of what the apps look like and how they work.

TweetDeck (TweetDeck.com)

In the world of social media desktop apps, there are few more popular solutions than TweetDeck. This application offers you some pretty significant benefits, and can help keeping up with your friends, followers, customers, clients or contacts far more simply than you might think.

Advantages: First, let's take a look at some of the advantages offered by TweetDeck. This app allows you to integrate an amazing number of social networks into a single location. You can use Twitter (obviously), but you can also add Facebook, MySpace, LinkedIn, Foursquare, MySpace and Google Buzz.

TweetDeck also allows you to schedule tweets and posts when you want them, which is great for those using social media to enhance their business. Retweets are also easier using TweetDeck, and following trending topics is also a cinch. You can even manage multiple Twitter accounts from this application.

Disadvantages: There really aren't any disadvantages to note about TweetDeck – it's solid, reliable and fully functional. It does what you want, when you want. Another great thing about this app is that there are versions for PCs and Macs, as well as for the iPhone, Android, Blackberry, and the iPad and there is even one built to run inside Google's Chrome browser.

Here's a screen shot of what you can expect with this app:

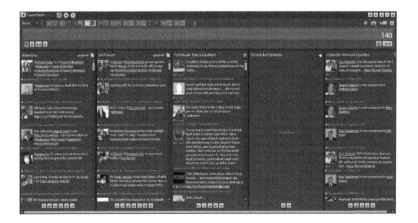

HootSuite (HootSuite.com)

HootSuite is an excellent option for those who need powerful features, excellent integration of other social networks, team collaboration capabilities, etc. This is the single best option out there for those who are using social media marketing for their businesses.

Now, admittedly, HootSuite is not a native desktop app. So why is it included in this list, then? Because you can make it a desktop app if you use a Mac – Fluid lets you run HootSuite (as well as Gmail, Facebook and even Pandora) as a desktop app right from your Dock.

For those who don't use a Mac, you can still find a HootSuite app, though you will have to run Chrome to use it – the Chrome app provides full functionality from your desktop. Mozilla Prism is another solution to turning HootSuite into a native desktop app.

Why bother? There are plenty of reasons to take the extra step needed to make this a desktop application.

Advantages: The most significant benefit of using HootSuite is that you will have access to powerful tools for marketing, tracking campaigns, managing your social media presence and so on.

You can also track statistics with real-time data, customize your interface, schedule updates when you want them and assign tasks to different team members. This is only the tip of the iceberg when it comes to the tools and functionality built into HootSuite. You can also use HootSuite from your Smartphone or your iPad, as well, with a native app designed for each platform.

Disadvantages: While there are no real "disadvantages" to using HootSuite, there are a few things that you should know before you leap into it. The first thing you need to understand is that while you can sign up to use HootSuite at no charge, the premium features do come at a cost. It's low, but it is something that you need to consider.

Another thing that you need to consider is the complexity of the program. While it is not difficult to customize and organize HootSuite to meet your needs, it can be a bit overwhelming at first. If you are just starting out with social media or third-party apps, then you might want to start off with something like TweetDeck or Seesmic until you have a bit more experience under your belt.

Here's a shot of what using HootSuite looks like – you can add streams from Facebook, a Facebook Page, LinkedIn, MySpace, Ping.fm, WordPress, Foursquare, Mixi and Ning.

Seesmic (Seesmic.com)

Seesmic is an interesting mix between HootSuite and TweetDeck. It runs in all browsers (Chrome, IE, Firefox and Safari), but is also available on mobile devices and as a desktop app. For now, let's focus on their desktop application.

In addition, Seesmic has become a one-stop solution for almost everything. There are currently over 50 different services that you can connect to using this application, with more on the way.

Seesmic is also quite easy on the eyes – its aesthetic is better than both HootSuite and TweetDeck, though the navigation is a bit different. Here's a rundown of the services that you can connect with via Seesmic:

- Formspring

- Facebook

- Foursquare

- Ning

- Klout

- Gowalla

- Twitter

- Last.fm

- YouTube

- Techmeme

That's a pretty long list, but you should understand that it includes more than just social networks. There are shopping, business, news, entertainment and utility plugins here, and many more. Seesmic Desktop also works on both PC and Mac (in addition to the multiple browsers and phone apps).

Advantages: There are some excellent advantages to using Seesmic, including the massive list of plugins and networks that come included. You'll also find that you can do most of the same things as in TweetDeck. (Seesmic is not quite as comprehensive as HootSuite in terms of business tools, though.)

Disadvantages: As with TweetDeck, there are really no disadvantages to using Seesmic, other than the fact that it does not update quite as quickly as TweetDeck does (TD offers real-time updating). Here's a look at how Seesmic will appear on your desktop:

There you have three of the best third-party social media desktop apps. Each of these has phone apps as well so that you can integrate your social media efforts (whether personal or business related) on all fronts. Now it's time to touch on a few other tools that can be worth your time.

Twitter Plugins

Twitter is still one of the fastest growing social networks in the world. Technically, this is actually a microblogging platform, but that doesn't change the fact that it has quadrupled in size during the last couple of years.

While you can (and should) use third-party apps to socialize or market via Twitter, there are some other tools that you should know about. These are plugins – they're accessible via the Settings and then the Connections tab on your profile page in Twitter (after you have signed up with them).

There are far too many plugins to list – they number in the thousands – but you should keep your eye out for those that offer decent functionality and results that cannot be achieved through Twitter itself. Here are a few good ones that you should consider, though you'll find lots of others in your own explorations online.

Who.Unfollowed.Me – This plugin does exactly what you think it does – it shows you who unfollowed you. It also allows you to track how many people have unfollowed you during the last 7 days, to check not only those who you are following but also those who are not following back and much more. The free version allows you to check your status every 15 minutes, but the paid version allows unlimited access. It's a pretty neat tool. I like to know who "unfollowed" me, but as a rule of thumb, I don't call folks out. I have had a few people tweet out that "@gasparem unfollowed me…"I don't get why they feel like they need to tweet it out to the rest of the world. I just like to know who is unfollowing me, and you might want to too, but don't be obsessed over it.

Twitpic – This plugin lets you post photos to Twitter through your web interface, as well as through TweetDeck and Seesmic. The "new" Twitter does allow you to post pictures now (and video for that matter), but many still choose to work with Twitpic.

Retweetist – This plugin/app lets you see what people are retweeting and who's doing the retweeting. This is a helpful tool for businesses using Twitter to market their products or services. Another feature that is also available within Twitter (you can click on "mentions" or click on "retweets" and "your tweets, retweeted").

Bit.ly – (notice I used bit.ly links throughout this book) This allows you to shorten URLs, as well as track and share them via Twitter. It also offers information like the number of times the URL has been clicked, as well as the most popular URLs. This is a great tool. The stats that you gain from using this tool are very valuable. Bit.ly should be used whenever you post any URL regardless of the size. Knowing where/when people are clicking on your link is key to knowing if your Social Media efforts are working.

Tweepz – Allows you to find followers and followees on Twitter based on topics, information, tags and other criteria that you specify. This can be useful for anyone, but especially for entrepreneurs and marketers, as well as those looking to broaden their follow/follower list a bit.

You'll find an incredible number of other plugins and applications that work with Twitter as you go about your normal online routine. Dropbox has a plugin for Twitter, as does Flipboard and Digg. Instagram, Yfrog and Twitzela are also excellent inclusions.

A Note on Toolbars

In general, browser toolbars are not always good things. If you install the wrong toolbar, you can find that your computer is compromised – inclusions like spyware and adware are pretty common here.

However, there are toolbars out there that are worth your time. Some of them are available even from your favorite social media sources – like StumbleUpon. Digg also offers an extension for Google's Chrome, so you can use this network right from the browser.

As always, be careful when installing toolbars – a large percentage of these are ranked as "badware" by leading Internet authorities. If you choose to install something like the StumbleUpon or Digg extension/toolbar, do so directly from the source or through your browser's app marketplace (most browsers have something like this).

Top Social Media Sites for You

Now that we have covered some of the best tools and the big 3 social networks, it's time to move on to some other social media sites. In this section, you'll learn more about what other top (less traveled) social media sites can offer you, as well as how they can be of use, whether you're a personal user or a business user.

StumbleUpon (StumbleUpon.com) – claims to have more than 8 million members.

StumbleUpon is an interesting social network designed to help you share sites and web content with millions of other people all around the world. Users of this network are called "stumblers." The core premise here is that you click the "stumble" button (via the site or via your toolbar/browser extension) and you are taken to a random webpage based on the categories and interests that you specify when you sign up with the service.

Once on a website, you can give it either thumbs up or thumbs down – you like it or you dislike it. Your votes are submitted to the network as a whole, as well as being recorded on your timeline. This is a great way to find some very interesting sites, excellent information and more, all while "stumbling" randomly around the Internet.

Of course, you can also interact with other people. You can see who has liked or disliked pages you visit and choose to follow them through the network, allowing you to send them messages, view pages that they have submitted and interact with them.

For personal users, StumbleUpon can offer hours of enjoyment and the interaction with other people that you want. For business users, StumbleUpon can also be of considerable value, allowing you to submit your own content to the network. The more people like it, the more visits your content, site, blog or page will receive.

Reddit (Reddit.com) **-** More than 1 billion pageviews per month, served to nearly 14 million unique visitors (stats from Yahoo News 2/3/11).

Reddit is a bit different. This network is similar to StumbleUpon in that it allows you to view pages submitted by others, interact with those users, read different content, and even submit your own.

One of the key differences here is the layout – Reddit is very basic looking but don't let that fool you. If all you want is an eye-catching layout, then Reddit is not for you. It's very basic. However, this lack of aesthetics allows users to do what they do best – focus on the content on each page.

Reddit is also immense – it's massive. It has just as many categories as StumbleUpon, but edges out the other media site in terms of user numbers. Like StumbleUpon, Reddit users can submit content, vote up or down on different items and they can leave comments, as well. You can also connect with other users on the network.

Unlike StumbleUpon, Reddit doesn't really give you much of a profile. It offers a preferences page where you can choose options like content language, comment options, media and others, but you put in very little personal information (which can be a good thing in many instances).

For personal users, Reddit can be a great way to find new websites, blogs, topics, etc. For business users, Reddit might not be so useful. However, for creators and entrepreneurs, as well as for those wishing to establish themselves in thought leadership, it can be a great tool.

Digg (Digg.com) - Close to 20 million monthly unique visitors (stats from CEO Matt Williams, Cnet interview 2/2/11)

Digg is very similar to Reddit, though it predates the other network a bit. Like Reddit, Digg is a news sharing site that allows users to submit content, vote up or down on the content and so on. However, Digg also offers a few key differences for users, and comes a bit closer to StumbleUpon in the way that it looks and operates, now that it has received its fourth update.

Digg users are given a personalized homepage that they are able to customize based on their interests and likes. News feeds (user submitted content) based on those categories are supplied on the homepage, and users can like or dislike content right from there. Users can also sort news based on age – they can choose the top in the last 24 hours, within a week or in the past 30 days.

For personal users who enjoy reading news and finding new content, Digg is an excellent resource. You can follow other users, see their top rated items, be notified when they vote up the stories and content that you have, and do many more things. For business users, Digg is closer to Reddit. That is, you can submit your own content for voting by the members, and it can be useful in establishing thought leadership, as well as in managing your brand.

Other Social Media/Networking/Bookmarking Sites

Obviously, the sites and networks listed thus far represent only a tiny fraction of what is available to Internet users, both personal and business users. As such, there are many other useful sites out there that can help you do, share and experience what you want. Below, you'll find a list of the top sites, as well as the category they slot into. (Unless otherwise noted, these are all .com.)

- YouTube – Video Sharing: (according to Youtube.com Fact Sheet) People are watching 2 billion videos a day on YouTube and uploading hundreds of thousands of videos daily. In fact, every minute, 24 hours of video is uploaded to YouTube. Their user base is broad in age range, 18-55, evenly divided between males and females, and spanning all geographies. Fifty-one percent of our users go to YouTube weekly or more often, and 52 percent of 18-34 year-olds share videos often with friends and colleagues.

- Flickr – Photos and Images: (as per Flickr.com blog post in September 2010) Flickr members upload more than 3,000 images every minute, and user "yeoaaron" uploaded the five billionth photo.

- Metacafe – Video Sharing: Metacafe is one of the world's largest video sites. They claim to attract more than 40 million unique viewers each month. (As per Metacafe's website). How is Metacafe different? (what they mean to other video sites, especially YouTube) Metacafe specializes in short-form original video content that is made for the interactive Internet medium. They don't have full-length television episodes or movies chopped into pieces. The average video on Metacafe is just over 90 seconds long.

- Scribd (pronounced "skribbed") – Articles/Books/Writing: According to Scribd.com, they reach 60 million readers every month. The site touts itself as "the world's largest social reading and publishing company." People have described Scribd as the largest book club on the planet. Anyone can join the conversation on any topic.

- Delicious (aka Del.icio.us) – General/News: A social bookmarking web service for storing, sharing, and discovering web bookmarks. The site was founded by Joshua Schachter (2003) and has since been acquired by Yahoo! (2005). In 2008, the service claimed more than 5.3 million users and 180 million unique bookmarked URLs. It is headquartered in Sunnyvale, California.

- Technorati – Blogging: Technorati was founded to help bloggers succeed by collecting, highlighting, and distributing the global online conversation. Founded as the first blog search engine, Technorati has expanded to a full service media company providing services to the blogs and social media sites and connecting them with advertisers who want to join the conversation, and whose online properties introduce blog content to millions of consumers Read more: http://bit.ly/eQiyFv

- Mixx – General/News: Founded by Chris McGill (Trouble-Maker-In-Chief), is a user-driven social media web site that serves to help users submit content or find content by peers based on interest and location. It combines social networking and bookmarking with web syndication, blogging and personalization tools.

- Slashdot (incidentally, I love the name of this site) – Technology: Slashdot was (originally a blog) created in September 1997 by Rob "CmdrTaco" Malda. Today it is owned by Geeknet, Inc. Slashdot serves about 40 million pages and 5 million uniques per month. It bills itself as "News for Nerds. Stuff that Matters", features user-submitted and user evaluated current affairs news stories about science and technology related topics.

- Gather – Writing/Articles: Gather.com is a social networking website designed to encourage interaction through various social, political and cultural topics. Freelance writers create more than 8,000 pieces of content, and reach about 9 million people worldwide. Members share their own views and can join in conversation with others who share similar interests. Its headquarters is in Boston, Massachusetts.

- Folkd – General/News: a social bookmarking and social news website that was founded in 2006 by Bastian Karweg. The website has grown into one of the biggest services of its kind and currently lists over 8 million public bookmarks by more than 500,000 users (May 2010). Folkd is available in 4 languages. Their strongest user base is in India.

- Posterous – Blogging/Photos: launched in July 2008 (because they "loved sharing thoughts, photos and videos with friends and family, but we didn't like how hard it was"). Posterous set out to make sharing as easy as sending an email. The site has grown steadily, adding new ways to share, and keeping their original pledge of simplicity. Posterous is funded by top-tier investors (Y Combinator, Redpoint Ventures, and Trinity Ventures). It is a very simple tool, and some very well known bloggers such as Mashable Editor Jennfier Van Grove and Edelman Digital's Steve Rubel have moved to it as one of their primary sources for information streaming. I am seeing it more and more as shareable links on Facebook.

Social Media Evolution – Where's It All Going?

As mentioned earlier in the book, the ongoing trend in social media of all forms is greater interconnectivity between different platforms. Nowhere is this more apparent than in mobile apps and apps developed specifically for use on tablets, such as Apple's iPad. Now, if you don't own a tablet yet, don't turn up your nose at this news.

Throughout the social media industry, more and more people are taking notice of the trend of mobile use. This applies to cell phones as much as it does to tablets and netbooks. However, look for the trend to begin centering on tablets more and more. Some experts expect tablets to begin replacing netbooks and even laptops for many users.

What does this trend of deviating toward the mobile market mean for you, the social media user? Actually, there are several implications. First, if you already own a tablet, or are actively engaged in using social media on your phone, then you can expect things to get easier and easier. More and more apps will allow you to log in via your Facebook or Twitter account, meaning that you have fewer details to keep organized.

If you are not a tablet or heavy phone user, you won't necessarily be left out, but there will be fewer traditional apps developed. The overall trend in the industry is one of moving toward "apps" as popularized by the iPhone and Android phones.

Don't look for that to change very soon. With the number of tablet models coming online, you might just find that your best defense is to join the gathering movement and start connecting via these handy devices.

Chapter Three

Tactics for Using Social Media to Market Your Business

If you want to harness the power and potential of social media for your business, it is essential to have the right tactics. While you might think that it is just as easy as choosing your sites, signing up and jumping right in (and it can be), there are some things that you should know before you join any network or service.

This chapter contains important information for business users, but you will find that many of these tactics can be employed by private, individual users who just want to make the most of their experience.

Why Do I Need Tactics?

You wouldn't launch a real world marketing campaign without doing a little research on the right method, the cost involved or the potential reach of the campaign, would you? Social media, networking and bookmarking are no different.

You need to have the right tactics in place before you jump in, or you might find that your results are a bit less than you might like.

The right tactics and, moreover, the right combination of tactics, are essential to achieve success in this realm. Not only will using the right methods and marketing tools help you boost your online presence and your profitability, but you can also boost brand recognition and ensure that your customers are able to interact with you.

The new age of social media is very different from anything that has gone before. Gone are the days when a business could be successful as a faceless, impersonal corporation. Today, consumers are demanding a personal connection with the businesses that they use.

In a way, this is a throwback to the days when "mom and pop" stores dominated the landscape. Customers knew the owners and operators; they interacted with them on a personal level.

Today, that trend has once more come to the fore, thanks in no small part to social media. Using the right tactics will help you capitalize on this trend and give your customers, clients and web visitors the experience that they want and expect.

If you're ready to find out the best ways to grab your customers' attention (and the attention of those on the fence), then here are the things that you need to know. To make things a little easier, the tactics have been broken up on the basis of the theme.

Listen, Listen, Listen

Listening is one of the most important things for you to do. This involves listening to your customers and clients, of course, but it also means listening to others in your industry or niche. It means reading, interacting and commenting when someone discusses you or your brand. How do you go about doing all this, though? Here are some simple tools and tactics to help you listen through social media.

First, you can use tools like Technorati and Google Blogsearch to build custom "ego" searches that will help you locate blog posts related to your company and your brand. This practice is also referred to as vanity searching or self-Googling. Essentially, you are creating automated tools that will help you locate posts that relate to you.

Once you find posts that talk about your company or that discuss your own posts, comment and interact with the audience and the author. Establish your personality and your expertise by interacting with others.

Another important tool is to make sure that you involve yourself with conversations about your company or brand on Twitter, as well. There are several tools that can help you do this, including Friendfeed. Third-party apps like HootSuite and TweetDeck can also help you locate these conversations on the Twitter network and ensure that you can get involved.

You will also find professional listening tools available for a premium price – Radian6 is just one example. However, the price of these solutions might be a bit too high for you. You'll be able to accomplish the same thing on your own for less, but you will have to spend the time needed to do it right.

Google Reader is your best friend in this area. You can use this tool to store those ego searches mentioned earlier and combine them all in one place. This allows you to access a central location for all of your information and will save you a bit of time, while still allowing you to find the posts and tweets that you need.

You also need to listen to others within your niche, not just those who are talking about your company, your brand or your blog posts. You need to follow thought leaders in your industry or niche. You need to listen to other business owners and innovators in your field. You can do this easily using podcasts, as well as creating custom searches for keywords on Twitter and interacting through other social networks.

Finding good podcasts is as simple as opening up iTunes (or your preferred marketplace, such as Android or Blackberry), and searching for podcasts in your industry. You'll find a rich landscape of different options, and you can learn from the best. Take the best of this information and share it with your followers, friends and connections via your blog, through Twitter, LinkedIn and Facebook. Don't forget to give credit where credit is due, though.

Create Your Home

You need to have a central online home for all of your efforts. This should be something separate from your Facebook or Twitter presence. For most businesses, this is a blog or website. You don't have to have a blog – not everyone does – but it is enormously beneficial. Having a blog allows you to achieve a number of things such as the following:

- Interacting with your visitors on a one-on-one basis

- Developing a personal brand

- Managing your brand through social interaction

- Giving your customers a new perspective of your business

- Highlighting your company culture through posts about events and other happenings

Of course, you need to make sure that you do a few things when you set up your blog. First, you can integrate the blog with your company's professional website. However, it might be useful to have it as a separate entity, so that you can enjoy the benefit of linking from the blog to your site.

If you choose to host your blog away from your main site, take the time to choose a good domain name. It needs to be easily spelled and remembered. It also needs to resonate with your customers and be relevant to your topic, your niche or your products, as well.

Invest the time (and/or money) required to have a nice design. While you will find a lot of great free templates out there, particularly if you use WordPress as the underlying framework for your blog, having your own customized theme can be enormously beneficial. This shows your customers that you are not just here for the short term, but that you intend to be around and you know how to stick it out.

No matter what else you include on your page, you need to have an "About" page. That page might be about you, or it might be about you and your company. However, no matter what its thrust is, it needs to be about you at the very least. This is the first step in giving your company a personal face and generating an image that will resonate with your customers.

You also need to give some consideration to your visitors. When building your blog, whether you use a premade template or invest in a custom design, you need to make sure that your site is:

- Easily navigated (You have to give your visitors simple tools to get around, or they'll head the other way.)

- Not loaded down with ads. (Ads can be great for revenue, but too many will distract your visitors and make it hard for them to focus on YOUR content.)

- Using easy to read fonts and colors (Stay away from bizarre, hard to read font/size/color combinations or your readers are going to run away.)

- Loading quickly (You cannot expect your visitors to wait an eternity for your page to load, so test it before you make changes and make sure that it loads quickly.)

Another important tactic is to make sure that you give your visitors several important tools. First, it should be simple for them to post comments on your blog posts. This encourages interaction from your visitors and increases your site's value. A blog that doesn't allow comments is one that doesn't want to generate a two-way conversation, and will quickly fail.

In addition, you need to make sure that you offer your visitors a quick, simple way to subscribe. A prominent RSS feed icon (linked appropriately, of course) is the best way to do this. Of course, you might also offer an email subscription as well.

Finally, you need to give your visitors easy ways to share your content on other social networks. You can add a "tweet this" button or a "share this" Facebook icon relatively easily. There are also powerful plugins for WordPress and other blogging solutions that can help your users share your content on many other networks. Here's a shot of one of the best out there – Sexy Bookmarks by Shareaholic (Shareaholic.com):

Ignore the text in the image above (it's from Shareaholic's website) and focus on that row of icons. When moused over on the website, each individual tab extends, and each is linked to the appropriate social media outlet or platform.

Having something like this at the bottom of each of your posts encourages your visitors to share your content where they like – where others will continue sharing it if they like what you have to say or share.

Of course, there are many other social bookmark and sharing tools out there. The one listed above is just an example of what you can do. Many WordPress themes today have their own social bookmark features built into their internal coding.

Get Your Passport

As has been mentioned throughout this book, you need to make use of multiple social media platforms if you really want to enjoy the utmost in terms of benefits. Using just one or two can offer you some results, but you'll find that having more social media outlets equates to better performance and success. Moreover, having accounts with some of these will make sharing and interacting simpler and easier.

You'll find that quite a few of the sites we'll cover here in a minute allow you to sign in with your Twitter or Facebook account. This can be a simple way to create accounts without having to worry about different logins for each. Of course, if you prefer, you're more than welcome to create an individual account with each service.

Of course, you need to make an account with Twitter and Facebook (You should also consider LinkedIn, especially if you are a business user.) These should be "givens", as you won't go far in social media marketing if you don't use them. You might also consider adding MySpace to that list, though this is totally up to you. MySpace does still offer some benefits, but an increasing number of consumers refuse to use the network; so you might not see much in terms of results from that particular venue.

In addition to those listed above, you should consider the following networks as "must have" inclusions in your social media marketing plan.

YouTube (Second largest internet search engine after Google.) is a vital one to include – video marketing has become enormously popular. If you want your marketing message or information to go viral, there are few better ways to achieve that than using YouTube. It's simple, powerful and has enormous scope, as well.

You should also consider using Flickr so that you can share photos. While there are many other photo-sharing sites out there, Flickr remains the most popular and is also one of the easiest to use. You can also consider Twitpic and Yfrog, specifically for sharing photos via Twitter.

You may also want to make an account on StumbleUpon, Reddit and Digg. These are excellent venues for sharing your content. However, you need to make sure that you do not generate the reputation of being a spammer.

That is, you need to submit content other than your own for the community to rate, rank and like. By submitting content other than just your own stuff, you make yourself a valued member of the community and encourage others to connect with you and rank your content.

Another good idea is to make an account with Upcoming.Yahoo.com. You can list upcoming events, happenings and things to do here. You'll find that this can be an invaluable tool whether you are creating virtual events that you want to boost attendance for, or hosting a real world event.

Finally, if you don't have a Google account (Gmail), then you need to get one now. This allows you to easily set up your Google Reader account, as well as taking advantage of Google's other tools, like Google Docs, Google Calendar, etc.

Reaching Out with Posts

Some marketers refer to the items covered in this section as "outposts" and the reason for that will become quite clear soon. You need to build the venues through which you will share your content with the rest of the world.

To do this, you need to know where your audience is – there is a very good chance that they're on Facebook and Twitter. MySpace might be a possible venue, depending on who it is that you want to connect with (You have a band, actress, actor, comedian.) LinkedIn is also a valuable venue, particularly for B2B companies and those seeking to grow their professional network.

You'll need to connect your RSS feeds (from your blog/site) to your various social networks. The most important one is Facebook – you can easily integrate your RSS feed here and lessen your workload. Double posting can become quite tedious, and doing this saves you time, while ensuring that you have content in both places.

You also need to make sure that you link to your social media presence on your blog, on your LinkedIn profile and in other places. Another important link to have is the one to your blog within your email signature. This helps you drive people you correspond with to your blog, and gives you yet another venue for developing traffic.

Your blog link should also appear on all of your social network/media profiles. That means you need to have that link on Facebook, Twitter, Digg, Reddit and anywhere else you can put it. Whether you have listed your blog with specialized blog services or not, you need to make sure that you have as many links to it as possible from your various accounts.

Hail to the King – Content, That Is

There is one undisputed king of the Internet – content. Content is what your followers, friends and contacts want. They don't want empty marketing hype. They don't want valueless posts that do nothing for them. They want viable, actionable, ORIGINAL content.

It is vital that you create new content for your blog and other venues on a regular basis. While by adding that RSS feed to Facebook and anywhere else you can/will help keep down your workload here, you HAVE to post fresh, real content frequently.

Does this mean that you have to post something new every day? Well, that certainly wouldn't hurt, but you don't have to be quite that frequent. However, you should post no less frequently than three times per week.

What's the point here? There are several reasons that you need to do this:

- Giving value to your followers: One of the most important reasons to post regularly is that you give your followers, readers and contacts additional value. This is the key to creating success – you have to give your followers value or they will find somewhere else to go.

- Give your followers something useful: By giving your followers information, tips, steps or tools that are useful, you increase your value to them. The more valuable they perceive you, the more you can expect them to promote you to their own connections and the more loyal they will be to you.

- Establish your leadership: You will also find that when you provide valuable, fresh, actionable content to your followers and readers, you are able to establish yourself as a leader in your niche. As you progress, you might even become a thought leader and be extremely influential with others.

What kind of content do you need to post, though? Obviously, whatever you post has to have value and use for your readers. However, you cannot post the same type of thing all the time. You need to vary it – mix it up. Don't be afraid to try new things. There are quite a few things that your readers will enjoy and find valuable, including:

- Tips

- How-to lists

- News

- Interviews

- Top 10 lists

- "Me too" posts – these often include information from another thought leader or influencer in your industry who allows you to expand and share

However, there are a few caveats to your posting. These are important rules that you need to follow to maintain and grow your reader/follower list.

First, be original. While "me too" posts can be valuable, you need to limit your use of them, as they are not technically original content. You can of course use them, but use them sparingly. As far as your top 10 lists and how-to lists are concerned, make them your own – be original.

Your readers value you for your information, for your perspective and for your expertise. Don't regurgitate the thoughts of others. Be yourself and be original in your content.

Another important point is to use some sort of graphic in as many posts as you can. This might be nothing more than your avatar, but studies have shown that graphics draw readers much more readily than text-only posts. The graphic might only have the barest connection with your post, but using pictures can help you reach out to more people and garner more interest from those who visit your blog, social network page and so on.

You should also keep your posts as brief as possible. While this doesn't mean condensing a 10-page post into a single paragraph summation, you do need to write with brevity in mind. Why is this? Internet readers do not have the same attention span as those reading traditional media. You have mere seconds to grab their attention, and you need to make your point relatively quickly.

Finally, consider adding some audio or video to your posts. Podcasts and vidcasts are excellent tools and can help you connect better with your audience. Doing this allows you to be more than just a faceless, voiceless "pen on the page."

It allows your readers (listeners/watchers) to connect with you on a visceral level and that's a good thing. You need to stand out in your readers' minds and using video and audio can be the best way to do just that.

Conversation – Building the Buzz

Unless you haven't been paying any attention, you know that social media is about conversation. It's about interacting with other people, whether those people are your friends and family, current clients or potential customers. To make the most of your social media marketing, you need to know how to start and maintain conversations to build buzz about your company or your brand.

How do you do that, though? If you're new to social media, then this can be the most daunting question of all. It can be hard to break out of the old-school marketing mold for many people. However, it is essential that you not only break out of that mold but that you shatter it so that you cannot sink back into it.

One of the first rules of starting conversations with social media is to read and comment on other people's blogs. This can build buzz quickly, and you will usually be able to leave a link to your own blog, website or other destination. That allows other users to not only respond to your comment, but also to check out what you're all about.

You also need to make sure that you leave valuable, relevant comments. Most people have seen spam comments on blogs that have nothing whatsoever to do with the post in question. Things like "I glad found such valuable info. I make sure share with other peoples," are pretty common. And if you think the typos and poor grammar in that example are extreme, you should read some more blog comments. These are spam, and they're HATED.

If you fall into this category, then shame on you. You'll find that this can get you blocked, and even ruin your reputation. It's a far better option to post real, viable, useful, on-topic comments. If you give real interaction, you're far more likely to get it in return. In addition, the more valuable and useful your comments are, the better they reflect on you.

Stay active in the discussions that you start or join. Once you comment, check back periodically and respond to any questions or comments directed at you. This not only gives other readers more opportunities to follow up by investigating your blog or site, but it shows that you are a committed, valuable member of the greater community (you'll find out more about "community" in the next section).

Your comments and interaction should also be humble – don't be a braggart. No matter what you do, there is someone out there who does it better. Remember this and it to tone down all of your online interaction. If you brag or make yourself out to be better than someone else, people will remember it and not fondly.

You can also create conversations across different blogs, across different social networks and so on. The key is to use links to help lead others to these different points in the conversation. Once again, this gives value and proves that you are in it for more than just yourself. In social media, you have to give in order to get. Always remember that.

Finally, you need to follow certain rules of conduct in your conversation, even with your own blog posts. For instance, do not delete critical comments simply because they criticize something. Reserve deletion for spam comments, those that use foul language and those that are offensive to others. If you delete comments that criticize, then you show that you are not really interested in what others have to say.

It's All about Community

See, here's that part about "community" that was mentioned above. Web 2.0 (social networking, blogging and the whole conglomerate of other platforms) is about creating a sense of community by interacting with other people. You need to foster this sense of community with your friends, followers, clients and customers. How should you do that, though?

First, you need to remember that social media is NOT about selling directly. This is not a marketplace; it is a community. You should never, ever attempt hard-sell tactics with your social media outlets or followers, as this will just alienate them.

Leave the selling portion of the equation to your homepage and make your social media efforts about generating a sense of community, a feeling of connectedness with your followers, "friends" and others.

You should also take the focus off of you to some extent. While you should certainly include yourself (or your business) in your social media efforts, you need to share the spotlight with others. Once again, this fosters a sense of community and offers greater value to your followers.

Your community consists of your blog readers, your followers on Twitter, your "friends" on Facebook, and your connections on LinkedIn (as well as many other individuals, of course, such as those on Digg and Reddit). You need to make it simple for your community to contact you. You don't have to give out your home phone number or your personal email address, but you do need to be reachable.

In addition, take time to thank your community for being there for you – thank individuals for their contributions, thank those who leave comments and those who help you with posts. Doing this not only shows that you are grateful, but that you are a real person. Being human is one of the most important aspects of using social media effectively, and there's no better way to do that than by thanking others.

Finally, if you screw up (and it's very possible that it will happen), apologize. Be sincere in your apology, as well. If you are to blame for the screw up, accept that blame and apologize to your community members. Again, this shows that you are human, but also that you are responsible, and this can increase your value to others.

Promote, Promote, Promote

Now, the title of this section might seem at odds with the rule imparted at the beginning of the last one, that you should never sell directly through social media. If you can't sell, then how do you promote?

Creative readers probably have an inkling of how to do this, but let's expound on the subject just a bit. How, exactly, do you go about promoting with social media without selling something directly to people?

The first rule of good promotion is; to use the social bookmarking tools available to you. Digg, Reddit and StumbleUpon have been mentioned several times thus far, and are vital for getting your message out. You can also use Del.icio.us, though the service has been declining in quality and functionality for a while now.

However, you should not submit everything to all sites; in, you should submit only those posts that are really worthy of immediate attention. If you submit everything, all the time, then you run the risk of looking like a spammer, something that must be avoided at all costs. You also need to make sure that you promote other people with these tools more than you do yourself. It comes back to you (trust me).

Consider doing guest blog posts on other people's blogs. This can be an excellent way to drive awareness, while still providing something useful for readers and even helping out others in your community. Invite others to post on your blog as well - it'll work out very well for you.

If you really want to maximize your promotional ability and your value to followers and customers, then you should also make use of YouTube. Making videos (with working links to your blog or other sites) can be very, very useful - you'll find any number of uses for videos. You can create how-to videos, tutorials, product highlights, funny videos, corporate culture videos, etc. The potential is enormous.

Don't neglect your status sections on Facebook and other social networks as promotional tools. While you can't sell directly through status updates, you can tease, inform, and incite curiosity very easily.

Finally, just being very good at what you do can be the best form of promotion. If you're worth it, others will help promote you.

Chapter Four

Tips for Social Media Users

Using social media effectively, means knowing what's what in the virtual landscape, whether you are a business or personal user. For those new to the world of social media, it can be a confusing, yet exciting place.

A few tips and pointers will help you enjoy your experience to the utmost, while helping you to avoid the problems that can crop up here. To help you get the most out of this chapter, it's been broken into two sections – one for personal users and the other for business users.

Personal Users – Social Media Tips You Must Know

For personal users, the world of social media is vast and filled with potential. Each different social network, bookmarking site, or news site holds the potential for enjoyment, knowledge and meeting new people.

Interacting with others and sharing what you enjoy are what this movement is all about. However, if you do not follow some simple tips, you might find that your enjoyment is a bit less than what it should be.

Your Safety: A Paramount Concern

It's hard to read the news today without seeing at least one reference to someone whose safety was compromised by their use of social media. While Facebook and Twitter can be enormously enjoyable, like the rest of the Internet, there can be threats here. It is vital that you take the proper steps to protect yourself and ensure your safety, as well as that of others.

Knowing Your Social Media Outlets

One of the first things you need to consider is the nature of the social media site or network in question. Not all of them are created equal, and you will find that some are better suited to your needs than others are. You might find it best to talk to friends and family about which networks and sites they use.

There are two primary reasons to find out who uses what here. First, it gives you someone to connect with right away. It can be very lonely joining a social network and not finding any connections right away.

While there are millions (perhaps billions) of people on these networks day in and day out, it can be tough to make connections at first. Therefore, having a handful of predetermined "friends" or followers can be a good thing.

Second, doing this allows you to find out more about the network and how it works. While you might like to be rather hands-on in the learning process (and that is the best way to learn the ropes), you should do a little research first. How do you set controls about who can read your posts? Does everyone on the network have access to what you post or are only authorized users able to see them?

Knowing more about social media sites and social networks before you leap straight in can also have some important ramifications for your safety. Safety is a critical concern for many people these days, not just with the potential for marketers to gain access to your personal information, but for hackers, spammers and identity thieves to do the same thing.

There is even concern that you might inadvertently provide information that can be used by those who want to harm you or your family. While this might sound frightening, there are things that you can do to enhance your safety – the next section deals with safety tips on social networks.

Safety Tips for Social Media Users

Ensuring that you, your family and your friends are safe on social networks is not that hard to accomplish. However, there are some specific things that you need to do (and not do) to have the safest experience possible.

- Phone numbers: While some social networks (like Facebook) give you the ability to list your phone number on your profile, that's probably a very bad idea. Not only can this information be sold to the highest bidder, but it can also fall into the wrong hands in other ways.

  It's very simple to do a reverse lookup on a phone number through Google and find your address and even maps to your home. That's not good news for those who post these things out there.

- Too much personal information: Many people post all their vital information on social networking sites. This is largely because they feel that their information is secure. That's wrong – your information is at risk anywhere on the Internet. There is a very good chance that any super-personal information you put online will fall into the wrong hands, and there will be nothing that you can do about it.

- Listing your location: What's wrong with listing your location on social networks? Actually, this can be part of the fun of using these services – Foursquare and other services like it work with your location to help you network and connect with others.

  However, there is always an element of risk in putting your location information out there on the web. After all, there is no guarantee that this information cannot be seen by others (those that you don't want to have access to it). For instance, if you list your address and then mention that you're going on vacation, you leave your home open for burglars.

- Once posted, it's always there: Many people think that if they post something and then delete it, it's gone for good. That's wrong. There are still versions of that information in existence on other people's computers. Therefore, think before you post, or you might be putting something out there that cannot be taken back.

- Be careful with the photos you post: While posting photos can be great fun, it can also be problematic. Any photo that you put online has the potential to be stolen and used in other ways. They can be altered by other people, they can be used in ways that you don't like and they might even become the property of someone else – check the privacy policy and usage guides of different social networks to find out what happens when you post information or photos to their site.

- Beware of physical meetings with online friends: Part of the enjoyment found when using social networks is making new friends and connections. However, when that friend or connection suggests meeting in person, be very careful. While it might be just as innocent as it seems, it could also be very bad.

  Predators can use social networks quite easily, masquerading as almost anyone to gain your trust. If you do decide to meet with that person, it needs to be in a very public place and you need to make sure that you inform other real-life friends about what you're going to do.

- Go with your gut: If you feel threatened by a user or that they are acting suspiciously, it's best to avoid them. You can report them to the site, and you can also warn others about them. Suspicious activity can include things like stalking, abusive messages, suggestive or lewd messages and so on.

- Set your user controls: Most social networks give you at least some control over who sees your posts and other similar information. For instance, Facebook gives you a wide range of different controls to limit or authorize people to see what you post.

  Twitter allows you to make your account private, so that only authorized followers can interact with you. Using these controls can be very important – make sure you know what your controls are set at and what happens if you leave them at the default setting.

- Watch what you post: Posting to your Facebook wall or tweeting away on Twitter can be a lot of fun. You get to share with others, comment on other people's posts, etc. However, you need to remember that everyone authorized can see what you put out there

– that includes your boss, your coworkers, your teachers, your parents – everyone.

Think twice before you post things that might be objectionable. If you want to be able to post whatever you want, then you should consider not authorizing users that might be offended or bothered by that information.

Profile Creation and Profile Pictures

Using the safety tips listed in the previous section, you will need to determine just how much information you want to share on your profile. Remember, while the information that you put on your profile will be publicly visible, the privacy settings on your profile will determine who gets to see it. Therefore, you might choose to put in a considerable amount of information and set your privacy settings to a moderate level to ensure that it is not at significant risk.

As a note, there is no such thing as "no risk" with the Internet. Any information that you put up could conceivably be found and used by those you don't want to have access to it. Therefore, you should still exercise caution here.

An alternate option is to put up only basic information (what might be available via public records) and set your privacy settings a bit lighter. As long as you remember not to put sensitive personal information on these networks, you can have a reasonable expectation of privacy.

You need to take care when choosing your profile picture as well. A simple image of you is fine. However, bear in mind that if you use a picture with others in it, they might not appreciate it. This includes family members, friends and even your children.

Quite a few people opt to use an "avatar", which is nothing more than an image that you decide you want to represent you on social networks. Almost anything will work here, from favorite video game characters to something a bit more abstract.

Obviously, if you are using LinkedIn, you will want to use a picture that is recognizable to potential connections, one that represents you. This is an essential consideration if you are using LinkedIn to grow your professional network for entrepreneurial reasons or if you are using it to find a new job (which can be done). When using LinkedIn (from profile creation to interaction), remember that it is about professional connections. It is NOT the same as Facebook. Keep that in mind when filling out your profile and choosing your profile picture.

Making Connections – Making Use of Social Media

Obviously, you're going to want to connect with other people on these social networks. The simplest and easiest way is to run a search for people that you know. All social networks give you the ability to conduct a user search. Most networks have a search bar near the top of the page that lets you type in what you want to find.

On Facebook, you can also use the search bar to find topics, companies, TV shows and other things that you like. By "liking" these pages, you open yourself up to new connections from other users, which is what Facebook is all about. However, searching for those you already know on the network is the fastest (and possibly the best) way to get started. Once you have been added to someone's friends list, you will be able to look through their friends and see if there are any other connections that you want to make.

Twitter is a little different, though you can still search for specific users as well as by topic. Again, the best way to start is by following those you already know on Twitter and then looking through their connections for any that you might want to follow in turn. Twitter is not as "real life" oriented as Facebook is, so it is completely acceptable to follow someone that you don't know – quite a few celebrities use Twitter (or at least have a presence on Twitter), and this might also be a good place to start.

In addition to celebrities, you will also find numerous comedians, authors, musicians, bands and other public entities that are not necessarily "companies" that you can follow quite easily. These can be excellent initial follows, at least to find out what is going on with them. However, don't be surprised if they do not follow you back.

Connecting via LinkedIn is just as simple, but you'll be limited to professional connections only. After all, that's what the network is all about. Rather than socialization with friends, LinkedIn is about making your professional network grow. They have a handy search feature that can help you find companies and individuals that you already know, and filling out your profile information completely will also help you make more connections here.

Using Social Media Etiquette Correctly

Now that we've dealt with some of the safety considerations, it's time to move on to another topic - social media etiquette. Social media etiquette is pretty important. It's also very different from what you might think. While some people feel that they can do and say whatever they want in these online environments, the truth is that you will have a much better time if you follow these few simple tips.

Of course, the proper etiquette to follow varies from network to network and from platform to platform. This section is broken down into specific segments to cover what you need to know about each.

General Etiquette Rules

These general rules of behavior should be applied to all social networks, bookmarking sites and other social media outlets. It's just good behavior, and you'll find that doing so helps you (and others) enjoy the experience more.

- **Give to get:** As mentioned previously, you need to give to get in these environments. You should give more attention to others than what you receive. This will come back to you.

- **Avoid flaming:** Flaming is simply the act of bashing others in comments or posts. Avoid this. Just because you're not face-to-face with someone, it does not give you license to act in this way.

- **Add value:** One of the best ways to ensure that you enjoy your experience to the utmost is to add value to the experience of others. Answer questions, make someone laugh or show compassion when needed.

- **Don't make enemies:** While it's not always possible to be Mr. Nice Guy, you need to try. Filling the environment with hate and spleen is a bad idea, and that will come back to you, too.

- **Respect others:** Follow the Golden Rule in social media environments, treat others the way you want to be treated.

- **Participate:** Actively participate in conversations with your friends, followers and connections. It will open up an entirely new world for you.

Now that we've established some broad ground rules (which can be summed up as "be nice"), it's time to move on to some network-specific etiquette rules. We'll start off with Facebook, since that's the most popular network and is quite possible that it will be your first experience with social networking.

Facebook Rules of Etiquette

Facebook is many things to many people. It is a way to stay connected with far-flung family and friends, a way to interact with friends outside of your face-to-face meetings, and more. However, you still need to follow some basic rules of behavior to maximize your use of this network. Here are some helpful do's and don'ts to get you started:

- **Do:** Add real-life friends and family that you want to connect with.

- **Don't:** Add people that you don't know until after you have introduced yourself. You can do this in the body of the friend request very easily. Don't be offended if someone declines your request, though. There's no rule saying that all friend requests need to be accepted.

- **Do:** Decline friend requests if you do not want to connect with someone.

- **Don't:** Send out mass invitations to games and applications on Facebook. Not everyone wants to play your games; so be judicious in the invites you send out.

- **Do:** Join groups dedicated to things that interest you.

- **Don't:** Spam your friends and family to join every group that you join.

- **Do:** Make real connections with people. Facebook is not a "who has the most friends" contest. Add friends that you really want to talk to and interact with.

- **Don't:** Use a fake name for your Facebook account. If you are a business, use a fan page, not a regular account. Facebook is about forming real connections between real people.

- **Do:** Keep private conversations private.

- **Don't:** Post sensitive information on your wall or on the walls of others. Respect your friends and family, and keep sensitive topics, information or communications to direct messages directed at only the recipient.

- **Do:** Share photos that you are comfortable with everyone seeing.

- **Don't:** Tag friends or family in unflattering or compromising photos, as this can have some very bad repercussions.

- **Do:** Untag friends and family from your photos if requested.

- **Don't:** Be offended if someone doesn't want to connect with you on a professional basis. That's what LinkedIn is for.

Twitter Rules of Etiquette

Just like Facebook, there is a lot to be gained by using Twitter. It's a great way to make new friends all around the world. It's also a good way to learn more about different topics, follow different trends and many more things. However, there are some rules that you need to follow too:

- **Do:** Follow people that interest you.

- **Don't:** Unfollow those people if they follow you back just to boost your count.

- **Do:** Connect with anyone whose tweets offer value, or who creates content you find interesting.

- **Don't:** Mass-follow everyone you can find just for the follow-backs to increase your own standing.

- **Do:** Tweet your thoughts and content.

- **Don't:** Spam – 'nuff said.

- **Do:** Request retweets of your tweets by adding "PLS RT" to the end.

- **Don't:** IM everyone on your follower list and ask them to retweet your messages.

- **Do:** Offer good content in your tweets that will get them retweeted even without a request.

- **Don't:** Stream nothing but your blog contents to Twitter. Participate in the conversation – that's what it's all about!

- **Do:** Add profile information and a picture to your profile page.

- **Don't:** Share too much information here, as it is public.

- **Do:** Interact with your followers on a regular basis.

- **Don't:** Tweet personal or confidential information out into the ether.

- **Do:** Retweet other people's content if it is worth it.

- **Don't:** Expect a "thank you" for every RT that you send out.

There are other considerations when using Twitter, but it's a bit more liberal than using Facebook. Many of the regular users here are entrepreneurs and will occasionally tweet their products or services. You can too, if you are a private creator. The important thing is to be respectful of others and to give before you get.

LinkedIn Rules of Etiquette

LinkedIn is a valuable social network if you want to make professional connections. Marketing with LinkedIn is certainly possible, but it is also of great use to individual users who want to grow their professional network. Of course, as with all social networks, there are some rules that you need to follow here:

- **Do:** Connect with people that are involved in your niche or industry.

- **Don't:** Harvest email addresses to create a marketing email list.

- **Do:** Connect with coworkers and others that you have worked with in the past.

- **Don't:** Ask for endorsements of your quality or skill from those who don't know you.

- **Do:** Recommend those who you know have the right skills or qualifications for a job.

- **Don't:** Spam everyone possible just to grow your network.

As you can see, the list of do's and don'ts for LinkedIn is a bit shorter than for Twitter or Facebook. However, many of the same rules do apply. Remember, this network is for professionals, but not for spamming. That is the single largest complaint from LinkedIn users – don't be that person.

Social News Rules of Etiquette

Social news sites like Reddit and Digg can be great places. There you can connect with other people, and find information, topics and things that interest you. These are not the same as social networks, but can still be very enjoyable for you. Of course, you have to know how to conduct yourself correctly here. The following tips will come in handy:

- **Do:** Share sites and topics of interest.

- **Don't:** Spam only your own content.

- **Do:** Rank and rate submissions from your friends and connections.

- **Don't:** Ask for votes if you have not given back first.

- **Do:** Submit topical, relevant stories (relevant to the topic of the category or the site).

- **Don't:** Submit stories that are not relevant to the site, the category or topic.

- **Do:** Comment on the submissions of others.

- **Don't:** Bury stories just to increase your standings.

- **Do:** Communicate when you disagree about content.

- **Don't:** Assume that someone who disagrees with you is launching a personal attack.

Social news sites can be great fun, and they can offer some serious benefits to those interested in finding new things, interacting with others who share the same interests and so on. However, you still have to use them correctly.

In Summation – Private Users

To sum up, you need to remember that social media is all about making real connections with real people. The basic rule of thumb in almost all instances is this: If you would not do something in real life, then why would you do it online? This applies to safety, to interaction with others and to how you treat your friends, followers and connections.

Business Users – Social Media Tips You Must Know

Just as in the case of personal users, there are some important tips on social media for business users. Many of these rules are the same as those for personal users and you really should read through the section preceding this one (if you haven't already). Of course, there are some specific rules that apply to businesses.

Which Social Networks Are Worth Your Time?

Before you leap headlong into social media marketing, you need to spend some time to determine which social networks are really worth your time. Surprisingly, not all networks are beneficial to all businesses. Moreover, the more you use, the more time you have to take to market, interact and post new content.

What are the best networks for you? To make that decision, you need to know a few things about each. We'll look at the Big 3:

Facebook: This one is excellent for long-term results, as well as for quite a bit of interaction. In addition to giving you excellent tools for finding new friends, Facebook also offers some interesting benefits for growing your presence on their network. If you don't use any other social network, Facebook is a "must" for any business user.

You'll find that creating Facebook ads allows you to put your message in front of a targeted audience, which is far better than mass marketing (targeted marketing offers a much higher ROI for a lower investment). You can also set your own budget for how much you'd like to pay per click on your FB ads, as well.

Twitter: As you have probably gathered from information from the rest of this book, you may already know that Twitter is not like other social networks. You don't have the same tools available to you here as with Facebook, and it's not geared for professionals the way LinkedIn is. Does that mean that this microblogging network is not worth using? It's quite the reverse, though it depends on your platform.

More and more people are finding the value of this network. It is excellent for creating real conversation in real-time. Unlike Facebook, you'll get almost instant responses when you tweet someone with a direct @. You'll also find that valuable content (your tweets) can go very far in just a short time.

However, Twitter is not for everyone. It is a very specialized medium and even those who are pretty savvy with social media platforms may take a little while to learn how to use. With the right approach, though, Twitter can be an invaluable aid for many people.

LinkedIn: LinkedIn may or may not be of use to you. As a social network for professionals, it does a great job of connecting you with others in your industry, or with companies in a related vertical market. However, it is **NOT** the same thing as Facebook, nor is it quite as useful as Twitter can be.

Does that mean you should automatically count this network out? The best thing to do is to try it out and see. If you are a B2B company, then it might be well worth your time. Even B2C companies can find some use here, as it can help you network with skilled professionals and grow your business network, even if it doesn't boost direct sales.

Important Tips to Maximize Your Social Media Experience

Before we launch into social media etiquette for business users (which is the next big section), we need to touch on a few important tips that apply to all social networks and social media platforms. These tips will help you maximize the value of your efforts and ensure that you are able to generate the personal image that you need.

A Note on Profiles

For personal users, the amount of information shared through a social network profile is completely optional. While less information might imply fewer friend requests, it can also be a safer decision. However, for business users, the situation is very different.

Your profile is one of the most powerful tools available to you, and you need to take the time required to fill it out completely. On a site like Twitter, this won't take very long at all. However, on sites like Facebook and LinkedIn, it will take a bit longer. Remember to fill out your profile completely on any social media site that you use, from Facebook to Digg.

Why is it so important that you fill out your profile? This is what people are going to see when they consider adding you to their network. Therefore, it pays to have the right information available for them. Does that mean you should stuff your profile with keywords? No – keep it low key and relevant.

Make sure that you fill out all the fields as much as possible on all profiles. You also need to remember to keep your profile personal. Most people will not be willing to "friend" a business on Facebook. Therefore, your profile needs to be about you. You can certainly attach your business' fan page to your profile, and you should. However, your actual Facebook page needs to have a human element.

A Note on Profile Pictures

Your profile picture is the image that your contacts, friends and followers will immediately associate with you on these networks. Therefore, it needs to be a good one. You can use almost anything, though you might want to stay away from anything that puts you in a bad light.

As a business user, your personal profile will affect how others feel about your business page. Therefore, if you have a profile picture that is "risqué" or has connotations that you don't want associated with your company, then you should probably choose a different photo.

For personal users, almost any photo they feel comfortable with everyone seeing will work. For a business user like you, though, you need to take a few other things into consideration. For instance, you should choose a picture that evokes the philosophy, core values and culture of your business. You might not even choose to have a picture of yourself – a picture of your business office or some other relevant thing will work.

You also need to make sure that your fan page has a relevant picture. Now, because the fan page will be directly about your business (rather than being about you and only indirectly about your company), you need to choose a profile picture that really represents what your company is all about. Remember, this image will be your "public face" on the social network you're using; so make it a good one.

What Type of Connections Should You Make?

The type of connections that you make on social networks and social media sites is very important, and will depend on a handful of different factors. These include:

- Your intended audience

- Your immediate goals

- Your business type

Let's address your intended audience first. This obviously applies to those to whom you want to market your business. This might be consumers, or it might be other businesses.

It might even be Internet marketing professionals. Your intended audience will be the single largest factor in determining what connections you make, both immediately and over the long term.

Your immediate goals will also play a role. For instance, if you are just starting out with a social network site, your goal might be to connect with others in your industry to broaden your reach. Alternatively, you might want to leap immediately into locating potential customers.

Finally, your business type will also determine the connections you make both right now and in the future. For example, if your company markets to Internet advertising professionals, then those will make up the bulk of your connections at all times.

As a note, the type of connections you make will also depend heavily on the network that you are using. For instance, on Facebook you might choose to connect with your end customers and potential customers. On LinkedIn, you might choose to connect with others in your industry, with complementary businesses and with members of your vertical market, as well as with potential customers.

On Twitter, you might choose to take another tack entirely. Here, you might choose to interact with individuals as opposed to businesses. You might decide that connecting with thought leaders in your industry on Twitter is the best approach, in order for you to benefit from the connection through more knowledge, retweets and direct mentions.

How Do You Make Connections?

The way that you make connections on different social networks varies. Facebook allows you to find friends through your existing connections, as well as through a search, which can include keywords, names, business names, etc. Once you have connected with someone, you can view their friends list and branch out from there.

Twitter is a bit different. The best place to start here is with a handful of known users – they might be industry experts in your niche, or they might be current customers. You can find more people to follow in a couple of ways on Twitter. One of the best is to check out the followers of those you follow or who follow you (yes, that's a lot of "follows").

However, you can also use Twitter's built-in search feature to find specific users, or to find tweets that contain specific keywords. For example, if your company manufactured piano keys, you could run a Twitter search for "piano", "pianos", "piano keys", "replacement piano keys" and the like. Once you find a tweet with that keyword, you can choose to follow the person who sent out the tweet.

Twitter also has a "Suggested" list that contains users who match your interests, share the same connections or have similar characteristics in other areas. This can be a very quick way to find people to follow that might be valuable additions to your marketing strategy.

Finally, connecting through LinkedIn is a bit different. You'll find suggested connections based on your industry, your previous and current work/business history, your location, education and more. You will also find that you can search for people by name or by company. Finally, other users will be able to find you through your profile information; so make sure that it is complete.

Your Facebook Fan Page

If you haven't already noticed, Facebook features pretty prominently throughout this book. This is because it is possibly the most important social network for business users. In almost all cases, you will find your audience here.

Now, as mentioned, you need to create a "fan" page for your business. This page can be connected to your personal Facebook profile (it really should be), but will act as your business' main presence on the social network. Creating a fan page is pretty simple. You just need to go to https://www.facebook.com/pages/create.php and click on the icon you want (celebrity, band or business, etc.). Here's a screen shot to help out:

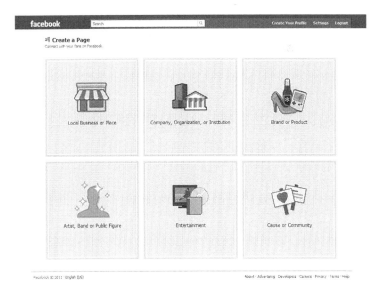

You can create a page for the following:

- Cause or community page (to support causes, topics, etc.)

- Local business or place

- Brand or product

- Entertainment

- Company, organization or institution

- Artist, band or public figure

When you click the icon link that represents the page you want to create, you'll see a few questions. Fill in the best way you can. Once complete you'll be taken to another page where you can put in more information on the page you want to create.

You also get the chance to give your page a name, "Bob's Bagels," for example. All you have to do then is click the button that says "Create Official Page."

Once you choose to create your page, you are given the option to create a new Facebook account (if you don't already have one), or to connect it with an existing account. If you have a personal account (you should), then you can connect it now and skip the rest of the signup process. If you don't, then go ahead and fill out all the information needed and then click the "Sign Up Now" button at the bottom of the screen.

From this point, you are able to customize your fan page the way you want. It's pretty similar to creating your personal page – you can upload a picture, fill out your profile information, write a bit about yourself and so on. You can also start marketing right away if you want, by using Facebook's ad feature.

It's a good idea to get some content up on your wall as soon as you can – preferably before you start inviting people to "like" your page. Speaking of that, you can do it very easily, just by choosing to invite friends and contacts from your personal page. Just one thing, don't just spam invitations to everyone. Only invite those who are going to be interested in what you have to offer.

Keep your wall updated with fresh information on a regular basis. You can connect your page to your blog and stream your posts to Facebook, but you need to do more than this.

You need to provide content specifically for your Facebook fans, and encourage interaction with them. When someone comments, comment back – strike up a conversation and show that you're a real business with a desire to connect with your customers and clients on a personal basis.

General Social Media Rules for Business Users

The following rules apply to all social networks and social media sites. The goal for businesses is the same as that for personal users – to connect, to generate conversation and to interact with other people on a PERSONAL level. Note that word in all caps there – it's very important. Just have a look at the following tips:

- **Give to get:** Just as with personal users, business users need to give in order to get. If you don't give attention, thanks and interaction to your followers, don't expect them to do it for you.

- **Don't spam**: Do NOT spam your friends, followers and contacts. Doing so is the best way to lose those people that you need. Spammers are not liked. In fact, there are movements in many social networks to ban those who practice this. On Twitter, you'll find it under the hashtag #TakeBackTwitter.

- **Participate:** Your friends and followers will talk to you through comments and through tweets. Interact with them, give them feedback and respond to their questions. Doing so is the best way to ensure that you are able to generate the brand image that you need to succeed here.

- **Add value:** You, as a business user, should be able to add value to your followers' experience. Your posts, whether on Facebook or Twitter, should contain content that appeals to your audience. It should educate, inform, make them think or make them laugh, depending on your audience, of course.

Facebook Rules of Etiquette for Business Users

Business users have some specific rules of etiquette to follow when using Facebook. These do's and don'ts can make a tremendous difference to how successful you are on this social network:

- **Do:** Create a profile under your name, not your business name.

- **Don't:** Use your business name as your name on Facebook (hopefully, you get the emphasis there).

- **Do:** Create a fan page and tie it to your personal Facebook page.

- **Don't:** Use your Facebook profile or fan page as a sales pitch. Facebook is about real interaction, remember.

- **Do:** Share content worth sharing.

- **Don't:** Hog the spotlight. Share the love and highlight other people.

- **Do:** Invite those who might be interested to groups you operate.

- **Don't:** Spam invites to everyone on your friends list.

- **Do:** Add those you know and those who connect with you.

- **Don't:** Add people without introducing yourself. Also, don't introduce yourself as your business – let your fans like your business page and keep yours for real interaction.

- **Do:** Interact with others on both your personal page and your fan page.

- **Don't:** Be offended or bothered when someone doesn't want to connect with your company on Facebook.

In general, business users should treat Facebook similar to how personal users do. Just remember that social networking is about interacting with others on a personal basis. You are more than your business or your business opportunity. If you fail to follow these rules of operation, you'll not have the success that you eagerly look for.

Twitter Rules of Etiquette for Business Users

Twitter is a great place for businesses. An incredible range of Twitter users are also business owners, entrepreneurs, creators and others who also market themselves through this medium. However, that does not give you carte blanche to throw the rulebook out. You need to follow these basic do's and don'ts to make the most of Twitter:

- **Do:** Humanize your profile by adding a picture that evokes your business and filling out your profile correctly. Make sure you link to your website or blog here, too.

- **Don't:** Stuff your profile with so many keywords that you look like a bot.

- **Do:** Follow those you think might be interested in your business or who are involved in your industry.

- **Don't:** Follow everyone and anyone just to grow your follower count.

- **Do:** Unfollow those who don't follow back.

- **Don't:** Unfollow people who have followed you just to make you look more popular.

- **Do:** Expect others to RT your content if it has value.

- **Don't:** Tweet things that have no value to your followers.

- **Do:** Promote yourself using Twitter regularly (though this should be limited).

- **Don't:** Promote yourself and only yourself. Make sure you promote the content of others, too.

- **Do:** Take an active role in the conversation with other people.

- **Don't:** Stream only the contents of your blog via RSS.

- **Do:** Request RTs of your content occasionally.

- **Don't:** Direct message followers to tell them to RT your content. If it's worth anything, they will anyway. If you have to message them to get it done, it's probably not worth sharing.

Twitter can be enormously beneficial once you get the hang of using it and develop a decent list of followers. However, abusing the network will only get you blocked. Twitter users do not like spam, as mentioned, and many have lost all tolerance for it. Spam at your own risk.

LinkedIn Rules of Etiquette for Business Users

LinkedIn is a bit more lenient than other networks, mostly because it's geared to help you connect with businesses and other professionals. It's not as focused on having an established real life, personal connection prior to connecting via the network; so you'll find that the rules of behavior are a bit different. However, these do's and don'ts are still important and you need to follow them or risk ruining your whole attempt:

- **Do:** Connect with those you know on a professional basis who use the network.

- **Don't:** Build a list of email addresses for marketing purposes WITHOUT ASKING the user if it is ok for you to do so.

- **Do:** Ask for endorsements from satisfied clients, those who know you well and others who have experience with your work quality.

- **Don't:** Ask for endorsements from those who do NOT know you and/or have never worked with you before.

- **Do:** Recommend those you know and those whose experience and expertise is fit for a particular position.

- **Don't:** Connect with anyone and everyone on the network regardless of their industry, location or professional connection to you or your company.

- **Do:** Start a LinkedIn Group that provides real value to its members.

- **Don't:** Spam invitations to all and sundry for your group, regardless of whether they will benefit or not.

As you can see, the rules for interaction on LinkedIn are a bit different from what they are for other networks. Still, it's important that you follow these rules. The most important thing is to avoid gaining the reputation of being a spammer. If you have that kind of reputation, then you will not enjoy your experience very much.

Social News Site Rules of Etiquette for Business Users

Social news sites can be excellent promotional tools for business users and entrepreneurs. You can use these sites to help spread the word, as well as to make new connections and learn a lot of useful things. However, using these sites incorrectly will have bad results. Follow these do's and don'ts to take maximum benefit from it:

- **Do:** Share interesting news and stories on a regular basis.

- **Don't:** Overload your feed. Try to share just one story per day per news site.

- **Do:** Promote your own news, stories and submissions regularly (though on a limited basis).

- **Don't:** Promote only your own stuff. Again, spammers are reviled everywhere, and <u>you do NOT want that type of reputation</u>.

- **Do:** Give votes to the submissions you find interesting and those from people with whom you have connected.

- **Don't:** Repeatedly ask for votes on your content from other users when you have never voted for theirs. Again, the rule of social media is "give to get."

- **Do:** Use comment fields to start conversations on the topic.

- **Don't:** Use comment fields solely for promotional purposes.

- **Do:** Submit interesting content to social media sites, content that is on target and on topic.

- **Don't:** Submit to random categories or off-topic information.

- **Do:** Give honest feedback on posts that you find interesting, or that you don't like.

- **Don't:** Bury or down-vote stories or items simply for the attention.

Social news sites like Reddit, Digg and StumbleUpon can be excellent tools when used correctly. However, it takes time to be successful there. Do not give in to the temptation to use underhanded tactics to speed up the process.

Chapter Five

Bringing It All Together

To have the best experience in using social media, whether you are a business user or a personal user, you need to know how to integrate everything into a seamless whole. You need to know how to bring it all together to create a single experience. There are several important things here, and this chapter will delve into each.

Step One

The first step is to choose your networks. As has been mentioned, different social networks have different things to offer – Facebook might be the first priority, but you'll find a ton of others out there. There are dozens of great sites that all offer you a way to interact with friends and family, customers and industry professionals. Take your time and choose the right sites for your needs.

As a note, don't be afraid to start small. If you are new to the world of social networking and social media, there's no need to sign up with 50 different networks. Not only are you far more likely to forget about most of them, but that's just too much to keep up with when you're starting out.

The best option is to choose a handful of networks to use. You might choose to use Facebook and Twitter, as well as Reddit and StumbleUpon, or you might opt for Twitter and LinkedIn. The possibilities are endless. However, remember the Big 3 – they're big and popular for a reason.

Using smaller social networks can be good, and can give you access to those who don't use the mainstream sites. However, it can also take something away from your experience. The less known a network is, the fewer people use it. Whether you're looking to connect with others on a personal basis or you want to market a new product or service, that's an important point to consider.

Therefore, take time to consider which networks will be the best for your particular needs. For personal users, it might be a very good option to find out what network most of your friends and family use.

This helps to ensure that you have an established base of potential connections already in place. It also ensures that you are actively engaged while you get the hang of using the network. Leaping immediately into a strange environment where you can't find anyone you know can be a lonely, frustrating experience.

For business users, a bit of research is in order here. You'll need to determine where, exactly your target audience can be found. Obviously, this is going to vary from company to company and platform to platform. Once you have determined where your target audience is, then you need to start building up your social media presence in that location.

Step Two

The second step is to create your account. This should be a pretty quick process, no matter what social network or social media site you're using. You do need to provide a valid name and email address, though, and in most cases, you will need to click the link in the authentication email the network sends out. This is a safety precaution designed to keep spammers and bots from creating accounts.

When filling out your profile and account information, make sure you bear the tips listed in the previous chapter in mind – both for personal and business users. Creating an account can be fun and easy, but keep an eye on the information that you choose to share.

On some networks, most notably Twitter, this won't be an issue, as the profile is very short. However, on Facebook, MySpace and LinkedIn, as well as on a few others, are capable of sharing almost every aspect of your life. <u>Only you</u> can determine if this is the right move for you. However, remember that any information you share, no matter what your privacy settings are, has the potential to become public knowledge. Choose carefully.

One important aspect here is to make sure that you link your blog or website to your profile page. Most networks give you the ability to do this. Some give you the chance to put in multiple sites, as well. This is very important for business users, but can also be a good thing for personal users with their own blog and/or website. If you have it, list it.

Step Three

Once you have put in your profile information, it's time to upload a picture for your profile. Personal users can usually get by without a picture, but business users have to have one. Even personal users can benefit from having a good profile picture in place, so long as it is one that they are comfortable sharing with everyone. Why is this?

First, if you don't have a profile picture, then you're not quite as authentic as when you have. Most social network users equate a lack of profile picture with being a spammer or a bot. Therefore, it's important to have some sort of image in place before you proceed further.

Take your time and choose a good picture. For personal users, this can be almost anything you want, from a cartoon character to a wedding photo. However, when you're first starting out, it's a good idea to have a real picture of yourself up. This will help other people recognize you. You stand a very good chance of connecting with people other than your immediate friends and family.

Facebook (and Twitter and LinkedIn to a lesser degree) lets you connect with people that you know but may have lost touch with. You can connect with college or high school friends that you haven't seen in years; so having a picture in place can be very beneficial.

If you don't have a profile picture, then you can expect to receive fewer connections. Again, this is largely due to the perception that those without a picture are "less real." Give potential connections a helping hand and choose a decent picture.

Finally, bear in mind the file size limits on your picture before you upload one. Most social networks will let you crop a photo to fit their size limits, but you should choose your picture with those size limits in mind.

Step Four

Now that you've got your profile up and your photo uploaded, it's time to start making connections. As mentioned previously, the best way to do this is by connecting with those you already know and interact with who use the network. You can simply ask those people (in the real world) if it would be ok for you to connect with them.

You can also use the search features of the various networks to connect with those you know, but whom you don't necessarily see on a regular basis – far-flung friends and family members, school friends, etc. Of course, you can also find interesting people to follow, but this is more applicable to Twitter than to Facebook or LinkedIn.

Be careful with your connections, and don't get your feelings hurt if someone doesn't want to connect with you. After all, there is any number of reasons they might choose not to make that particular connection.

A lot of folks prefer to keep their social media usage to close friends and family and, if you don't fall in that tight-knit circle, they don't want to connect. Others might simply have missed your friend request or follow notification. Thus, not making a connection is not a snub, and it is not cause for you to feel slighted or ignored.

Step Five

After you've made some connections, it's best to just use the network for a little while. Get to know how the network operates, what you can do and make more connections before you do anything else. Becoming familiar with how things work before you change tacks is always a good idea and will also help you in the next step.

For many people, it can take days or even weeks to become familiar with all that you can do on these networks. This is especially true if you only use them every now and then. It is definitely in your best interest to learn the ropes before you take on another project, such as learning how to use a third-party program like TweetDeck or HootSuite.

Step Six

This is not a necessity, but if you use more than one social network, you'll find it can be of immense benefit. As outlined previously, you'll find that third-party apps can be very handy here. Consider programs like TweetDeck, HootSuite and Seesmic to help you stay connected to all of your social networks at the same time.

This can be of serious benefit to business users who need to integrate a marketing plan across several different platforms, but it can also benefit the casual personal user who enjoys interacting in more than one place.

With a good third-party app, you can easily keep track of conversations between friends, post new things to each or the same post to several networks at the same time. The level of control this gives you is immense, and should not be underestimated. Using the right application can help you streamline your entire social media experience.

There are also services like FriendFeed.com that can help you achieve similar results. FriendFeed helps you combine Facebook and Twitter friends, as well as allowing you to invite those from your Yahoo! Mail or Hotmail account and then interact with everyone in a single setting via a web interface.

Step Seven

Picking the social media sites (Digg, Reddit, etc.) that you want to use is the next step. It's advisable that you leave this for last, particularly if you are new to all forms of social media. The learning curve gets steeper the more things you attempt to learn at one time, so start with Facebook and Twitter, and then work your way up to other social media sites.

Probably you are familiar with several of these already – most people have at least watched a video or two on YouTube and you have probably read or even commented on someone's blog post in the past. Still, the best course of action is to integrate things slowly to help make sure that you are able to maximize your use of these different tools.

By taking it a bit slowly, you learn how to use each different network or site to the fullest before you slap another learning experience on top of it. That goes a long way toward making your experience better, and ensuring that you are able to get the best results out of it, the results that you want.

Summary

Boy that was a lot to swallow! Things are changing weekly, if not daily. The world of social media is an exciting one. The current climate is a lot like the days of the Dot Com boom. It was a fun time, and websites were becoming more and more innovative with each passing month. With growth came a sleuth of scammers trying to take advantage of unknowing consumers and businesses.

Every few weeks I hear from someone that overpaid for Social Media Marketing services and got burned. I do my best to expose these folks when I can, but it's not easy. Hopefully this book will arm you with information to confront these frauds. Beware of the ones with badges such as a "Certified Social Media" this or an "Official Social Media" that. Someone who takes a week long course is by no means as "expert".

Even if you absorb nothing else from this book, just keep in mind that it's all about <u>relationships</u>.

Remember:

1) Be **GENUINE!**

2) It's not always about you/your business

3) Make sure to create social participation within your organization

I invite you to contact me any time you have a question (email me or use my Formspring link below). I may not always have the answer, but I can at least point you in the right direction. Have fun, and remember I want you to *Socialize With Me*!

Follow Me: Twitter.com/gasparem

Friend Me: Facebook.com/gasparem

Connect Me: Linkedin.com/in/gasparem

Ask Me: Formspring.com/gasparem

Web: http://www.gaspare.me

Acknowledgments

I would like to take a moment to thank all the people that helped make this book a better book (and many did not even know they were helping).

First, my beautiful wife and children. Lisa you have the patience of a saint. You knew nothing of this book. I had to fit in writing late at night, here and there during the weekends. Isabel and Josh, I will make sure to take you to Chuck-E-Cheese a few more times this summer to make up for lost time.

Ben Hoffman, you take a beating from me over the phone (and now Skype) almost every day, but you never take personal offense at my wise cracks. Thank you for all your hard work. You deserve way more than I can ever pay. You and Jen run TSCinternet.com better than I ever did. Your design ideas give my work the much needed razzle dazzle.

My family. Mom, dad, Nona, my brother-in-law Marc, my sister Lina and her kids (Steven, Jason, and Andrew). Thanks for all the times you picked up my kids from school and baby sat while I was away. Traveling is never easy but with your help you made my life (and Lisa's) much easier.

All my online Friends/Fans/Contacts/Group Members – You guys are the best. I truly feel a connection with many of you. It's a wonderful feeling that I could land in Norway, Italy, France, England (anywhere around the globe really) and have a friend to help me navigate. The 12,000 plus (as of this printing) members of the Maritime Network on Linkedin.com. Thanks to my fellow "Rosedalians". I started the "Growing Up in Rosedale" with 10 friends, and the group has blossomed to over 2,800 members (friends).

Special Thanks:

Dani Brabaw

Glen Justice

Dr. P J George

Keith Schwartz

Bert Cohen

Dan Collender

Nick Fineman

Jack Frost (my dog)

My 80's playlist (you kept me company many a long night)

Glossary

A

Adsense: Google Adsense is a pay-per-click advertisement application which is available to bloggers and web publishers as a way to generate revenue from the traffic on their sites. The owner of the site selects which ads they will host and Adsense pays the owner of the site each time an ad is clicked.

Aggregator: these are Internet based tools and applications which gather content provided via RSS feeds from many different websites and display the content in one central location. Google Reader is an aggregator.

Akismet: an application for blogging platforms, such as WordPress, functioning as a filter for trapping link Spam and other forms of undesirable content contributions from visitors.

Alerts (Google): search engines allow you to specify words, phrases or tags that you want checked periodically, with the results of those searches returned to you by email. You may also be able to read the searches by RSS feed. This form of search allows you to check whether you, your organization, your blog or blog item have been mentioned elsewhere, and so to respond if you wish.

Archive: an archive is an online conversation which is no longer open for additional comment but is available for future reference. Most blogs keep an archive where visitors can view older posts.

Avatar: avatars are graphical representations of real people. Avatars can be two dimensional images, representing the author of a blog or micro-blog; or, they can be three dimensional figures, occupying space in a virtual world.

B

Blog: weblogs or "blogs" are websites hosting content that is self-published, typically by the owner of the site (blogger). Blogs keep a record of all content updates which are posted to the site in reverse-chronological order (thus the original term, web-logs). Visitors can view the updates on the site or on an aggregator, via RSS feeds.

Blogger: bloggers are individuals who generate content for blogs, either as a pastime or professionally. Professional bloggers sometimes generate levels of esteem and prestige comparable to that of journalists.

Blogroll: a blogroll is a list of similar or recommended blogs that a blogger will list on his or her blog.

Blogosphere: is the term used to describe the totality of blogs on the Internet, and the conversations taking place within that.

Bookmarking: bookmarking means to save a website address for future reference. This can be done individually on an Internet browser, such as Mozilla Firefox. An address can also be bookmarked through a social bookmarking site, such as del.icio.us. Social bookmarking allows visitors to comment on and rate the content that is stored there. Other social bookmarking sites include Digg, StumbleUpon and Mixx.

Bulletin boards: were the early vehicles for online collaboration, where users connected with a central computer to post and read email-like messages. They were the electronic equivalent of public notice boards. The term is still used for forums.

C

Categories: categories are ways to organize content on a site. Blogs often organize their archive into categories which group older posts by topic.

Chat: is interaction on a web site, with a number of people adding text items one after the other into the same space at (almost) the same time. A place for chat – chat room – differs from a forum because in chat, conversations happen in "real time", rather as they do face to face.

Collaboration: collaboration is a Web 2.0 concept that the contribution of large numbers of individuals, using social media tools, is what drives quality content on the Internet.

Collective Intelligence: the human idea that a community or group of individuals is capable of higher thought processes than an individual. Social media applications of this concept include online communities which provide user-created informative content, such as Wikipedia.

Comments: Comments are content generated by individuals who have read a blog and are usually posted below the blog entry. Comments can often be vehicles for creating advanced levels of discussion and increase the lifespan of blog posts.

Congoo: Congoo is a news sharing social network that offers free subscription content across hundreds of broad and niche topics.

Connections: please refer to "friends."

Content: Any text, image, video or other created material published on the internet.

Crowd Sourcing: crowd sourcing is the process used by many social bookmarking sites where individuals are allowed to "vote" on news stories and articles to determine their value and relevance within the site. Crowd sourcing is driven by other social media concepts, such as collaboration and collective intelligence.

D

Dashboard: the dashboard refers to any area of administrative control for operating social media applications, such as blogging software or a social media user profile.

Delicious: Del.icio.ous is a popular social bookmarking site which allows members to share, store and organize their favorite online content.

Digg: Digg is a popular social bookmarking and crowd sourcing site.

E

Ego searches: See alerts

Entry: an entry refers to a post made on a blog or micro-blog.

Email: Electronic mail is messages transmitted over the Internet. These may be simply text, or accompanied by attachments like documents, images or other content.

Email lists (or groups): are important networking tools offering the facility to "starburst" a message from a central postbox to any number of subscribers, and for them to respond. Lists usually offer a facility for reading and replying through a web page - so they can also operate like forums. This web page may offer an RSS feed - so joining up old and new tools. However, there is something of a divide between blog-based conversations and those on lists and forums because the former are dispersed across a network and the latter don't usually allow tagging or such easy linking.

F

Face-to-face (f2f): is used to describe people meeting offline. While social media may reduce the need to meet, direct contact gives far more clues, quickly, about a person than you can get online. Online interaction is likely to be richer after f2f meetings.

Facebook: Facebook is a popular social networking site which gives free -access. Facebook was initially limited to students with a college email domain but has since expanded to be available to anyone 13 years of age or older.

Facilitator: is someone who helps people in an online group or forum manage their conversations. They may help agree a set of rules, draw out topics for discussion, gently keep people on topic, and summaries.

Flickr: Flickr is a media hosting network where users can upload and share image files.

Forums: Forums are areas on a website which are dedicated to facilitating conversation through comments and message boards.

Friends: friends, or connections, are individuals who agree to link to one another's profile on a social networking site, such as Facebook or MySpace.

G

Groups: groups are micro-communities within a social networking site for individuals who share a particular interest.

H

Hashtag (#): hashtags are placed in front of words to tag or categorize a post. Hashtags are used on Twitter to group tweets and more easily follow discussion topics.

I

Instant Messaging: instant messaging is a service where individuals can communicate through a real time, text-based exchange over the Internet.

K

Kaboodle: Kaboodle is a social shopping network where members find, suggest and share products.

L

LinkedIn: LinkedIn is a social networking site. Much like Facebook, LinkedIn allows members to connect with other users on the network, although LinkedIn is geared more toward professional connections.

Links: are the highlighted text or images that, when clicked, jump you from one web page or item of content to another. Bloggers use links a lot when writing, to reference their own or other content. Linking is another aspect of sharing, by which you offer content that may be linked, and acknowledge the value of other's people's contributions by linking to them. It is part of being open and generous.

Listening: in the blogosphere it is the art of skimming feeds to see what topics are bubbling up, and also setting up searches that monitor when you or your organization is mentioned.

Location: the nature of location and presence has been revolutionized by the Internet and social media, because you can be active online in many different places, including in virtual   worlds.

Logging in: is the process of gaining access to a website that restricts access to content, and requires registration. This usually involves typing in a username and password. The username may be your "real" name, or a combination of letters and/or numbers chosen for the purpose.

Lurkers: are people who read but don't contribute or add comments to forums. The rule-of-thumb norm suggests that about one per cent of people contribute new content to an online community, another nine percent comment, and the rest lurk. However, this may not be a passive role because content read on forums may spark interaction elsewhere.

M

Micro-blog: a micro-blog is a social media utility where users can share small status updates and information. Micro-blogs combine aspects of blogs (personalized web posting) and aspects of social networking sites (making and tracking connections, or "friends").

MySpace: MySpace is a social networking community. MySpace allows more freedom for users to personalize their profiles than other social networking sites, such as Facebook, which are more structured.

N

Ning: Ning is a hosting service with a set of community building tools that allows anyone to create their own social network.

O

Open-source software: open-source software is computer software with a special license which allows users to edit and improve the source code. Open-source software is an example of the kind of collaboration that is encouraged under Web 2.0.

P

Peer-to-peer: peer-to-peer refers to any type of interaction between two or more people within a specific social network. Quite often the term is associated with file sharing.

Podcast: a podcast is audio or video content which can be downloaded and listened to or viewed offline. Podcasts are often created to provide copies of radio or television programming, as well as to accompany Internet press releases.

Profile: a profile is a personal page within a social network created by a user. The profile provides information about the user and often links to the profiles of the user's friends.

R

Registration: registration refers to the process of signing up to participate in an online social media network or community.

RSS: RSS stands for Really Simple Syndication (or Rich Site Summary). RSS feeds allow users to subscribe to content updates on their favorite blogs and websites.

S

SlideShare: SlideShare is a presentation and document sharing social network.

Sphinn: Sphinn is a niche social bookmarking website for online marketers.

Squidoo: Squidoo consists of easy to build, single page website, or lenses, created by members on a variety of topics.

Social Media: social media refers to all online tools that are available for users to generate content and communicate through the Internet. This includes blogs, social networks, file hosting sites and bookmarking sites.

Social Network: a social network is a site or community on the Internet where members can interact with one another and share content.

Social networking: sites are online places where users can create a profile for themselves, and then socialize with others using a range of social media tools including blogs, video, images, tagging, lists of friends, forums and messaging.

Stories: Stories as well as conversations are a -strong themes in blogging. Anecdotes, bits of gossip and longer narratives work particularly well on blogs if they have a personal angle. It helps others get to know the blogger - and helps the blogger find and extend their voice

Subscribing: subscribing is the process of adding an RSS feed to an aggregator.

T

Tags: tags are a list of keywords which are attached to bookmarked content, a blog post or a media file. The tags are used to help categorize the content.

Technorati: Technorati is a leading blog search engine.

Teleconference: a teleconference is where a meeting takes place virtually and the attendees might be in completely different locations. Teleconferencing takes advantage of a number of different social media tools, including VOIP and instant messaging. GoToMeeting is an example of teleconferencing software.

Troll: A hurtful but possibly valuable loser who, for whatever reason, is both obsessed by and constantly annoyed with, and deeply offended by everything you write on your blog. You may be able to stop them commenting on your blog, but you can't ban them from commenting on other sites and pointing back to your blog, and you can't ban them from posting things on their own blog that point back to your site.

Tweet: a tweet refers to an entry made on the micro-blogging site, Twitter. Tweets can be status updates, links or information and can even include links and can be up to 140 characters long.

Tweetup: a Tweetup is a meetup organized for friends and strangers on Twitter.

Twitter: Twitter is a micro-blogging platform which allows users to create profiles and follow other users as friends, much like a social networking site.

U

User-generated Content: User-generated content refers to any piece of content created intentionally for free distribution on the Internet.

Usenet: A distributed bulletin board system developed in the early days of the Internet. Newsgroups are sometimes referred to as USENET forums.

V

Voice (AKA "your voice"): online social media enables you to extend your voice by increasing your reach across the internet, and doing that in the way that suits you best. You can write - or if you are a visual person you can upload photos or other images and invite comments. If you prefer talking, use Voice over IP (Skype), or perhaps record and upload a podcast, or capture interviews and events on video (JustinTV). Your voice can be focused on your blog ... or be available on other sites through your commenting, linking and use of social media websites.

VOIP: VOIP is an acronym for Voice Over Internet Protocol. VOIP allows a user to make phone calls through a computer with an Internet connection (think Skype).

W

Web 2.0: Web 2.0 refers to the term used to describe the rise in the popularity of blogs, file hosting and other social networking sites. Web 2.0 is a belief that the Internet should be used as a public access platform and less as a vehicle for publishing. Principles of Web 2.0 include collaboration, crowd sourcing and open-source software.

Wiki: a wiki refers to any page or collection of pages on the Internet that can be edited by visitors. Wikis are examples of collaboration.

Wikipedia: Wikipedia is a free encyclopedia consisting of user-generated content. Wikipedia is administered by the Wikimedia Foundation, a not-profit group.

Wetpaint: Wetpaint combines aspects of wikis, blogs, forums and social networks so that anyone can create and share online content.

Y

YouTube: YouTube is a popular video hosting site. Users can view, upload and comment on video content for no charge.

Yahoo! Answers: Yahoo! Answers is an online community where anyone can ask a question on any topics and get immediate answers from real people.

#: the "#" symbol is called a hashtag.

Recommended Reading

Below is a list of great books on the topic of Social Media, Business, PR, Consulting, and Marketing:

1) Social Media 101 by Chris Brogan

2) Tell To Win by Peter Guber

3) Don't Make Me Think by Steve Krug

4) Facebook Marketing by Steven Holzner

5) Branding Only Works On Cattle By Jonathan Salem Baskin

6) Full Frontal PR by Richard Laermer

7) Million Dollar Consulting by Alan Weiss

8) Bag the Elephant! by Steve Kaplan

9) Hug Your Customers by Jack Mitchell

10) The New Rules of Marketing & PR by David Merrman Scott

Works Cited

Find, manage Facebook friends without frustration - TODAY (n.d.). Retrieved from http://today.msnbc.msn.com/id/41629447/ns/today-today_tech/

LinkedIn - About Us. (n.d.). Retrieved from http://press.linkedin.com/about/

Facebox facts - Freebase. (n.d.). Retrieved from http://www.freebase.com/view/en/facebox

YouTube Demographics Round-Up :: Elites TV. (n.d.). Retrieved from http://elitestv.com/pub/2009/07/youtube-demographics-round-up

Web 2.0 video clips sharing community - Metacafe. (n.d.). Retrieved from http://www.metacafe.com/aboutUs/

About Technorati - Technorati. (n.d.). Retrieved from http://technorati.com/about-technorati/

Mixx facts - Freebase. (n.d.). Retrieved from http://www.freebase.com/view/en/mixx

Slashdot - Wikipedia, the free encyclopedia. (n.d.). Retrieved fromhttp://en.wikipedia.org/wiki/Search?search=Slashdot

glossary of social media - Sniki Wiki Social Media List. (n.d.). Retrieved from http://sniki.org/glossary-of-social-media/

Links

Below are some useful links in your quest for knowledge and some that are just plain fun!

1) http://www.mashable.com

2) http://allthingsd.com

3) http://www.wired.com

4) http://www.techcrunch.com

5) http://www.geek.com

6) http://www.techrepublic.com

7) http://www.wired.com/wiredscience

8) http://www.abovetopsecret.com

9) http://www.donorschoose.org

10) http://www.donothingfor2minutes.com

11) http://www.livegreenrewards.com